Authority and Power in Social Interaction

Authority and Power in Social Interaction explores methods of analyzing authority and power in the minutiae of interaction. Drawing on the expertise of a diverse international team of organizational communication and language and social interaction scholars, this book suggests reverting the perspective that notions of authority and power constrain human activity, to determine how people (re)create them through conversation and other joint action.

Confronting several perspectives within each chapter, the book offers a broad range of approaches to each theme: how and when to bring "context" into the analysis, formal authority, institutions, bodies and materiality, immateriality, and third parties. A core belief of this volume is that authority and power are not looming over human activity; rather, we weave together the constraints that we mutually impose on each other. Observing the details of how this joint process takes place may at once better account for how authority and power emerge and impact our actions, and provide guidelines on how to resist them.

This book will be an important reference for students and scholars in language and social interaction, organizational communication, as well as those interested in an alternative take on issues of authority and power. It will also find resonance among those interested in managements studies, public administration and other disciplines concerned with situations where authority is a crucial issue.

Nicolas Bencherki is an associate professor of organizational communication at TÉLUQ Montréal. His research focuses on the intersecting roles of organizational communication and materiality in the interactional constitution of membership, strategy and other conventional organizational issues in the setting of non-profit and community-based organizations, with a special interest for the concept of property.

Frédérik Matte is an assistant professor of communication at University of Ottawa, Canada. He studies tensions in the extreme and emergency situations faced by international non-governmental organizations (INGOs). He is interested in patient caring relationships, organizational change, intercultural settings and multi-lingual environments as well as ethical issues.

François Cooren, PhD, is a professor at the Université de Montréal, Canada. His research focuses on organizational communication, language and social interaction, as well as communication theory. In 2010–2011, he was the president of the International Communication Association (ICA) and was elected fellow of this association in 2013. He is also the current president of the International Association for Dialogue Analysis (IADA, 2012–2019), as well as a Distinguished Scholar of the National Communication Association.

Routledge Studies in Communication, Organization, and Organizing

Series Editor:
François Cooren

The goal of this series is to publish original research in the field of organizational communication, with a particular—but not exclusive—focus on the constitutive or performative aspects of communication. In doing so, this series aims to be an outlet for cutting-edge research monographs, edited books, and handbooks that will redefine, refresh and redirect scholarship in this field.

The volumes published in this series address topics as varied as branding, spiritual organizing, collaboration, employee communication, corporate authority, organizational timing and spacing, organizational change, organizational sense making, organization membership, and disorganization. What unifies this diversity of themes is the authors' focus on communication, especially in its constitutive and performative dimensions. In other words, authors are encouraged to highlight the key role communication plays in all these processes.

Methodological and Ontological Principles of Observation and Analysis
Following and Analyzing Things and Beings in Our Everyday World
Edited by François Cooren and Fabienne Malbois

Dis/Organization as Communication
Exploring the Disordering, Disruptive and Chaotic Properties
of Communication
Edited by Consuelo Vásquez and Tim Kuhn

Authority and Power in Social Interaction
Methods and Analysis
Edited by Nicolas Bencherki, Frédérik Matte and François Cooren

For more information about this series, please visit: www.routledge.com/
Routledge-Studies-in-Communication-Organization-and-Organizing/
book-series/RSCOO

Authority and Power in Social Interaction
Methods and Analysis

Edited by Nicolas Bencherki,
Frédérik Matte and François Cooren

Routledge
Taylor & Francis Group

LONDON AND NEW YORK

First published 2020 by Routledge

2 Park Square, Milton Park, Abingdon, Oxon OX14 4RN
605 Third Avenue, New York, NY 10017

Routledge is an imprint of the Taylor & Francis Group, an informa business

First issued in paperback 2021

Publisher's Note

The publisher has gone to great lengths to ensure the quality of this reprint but points out that some imperfections in the original copies may be apparent.

Library of Congress Cataloging-in-Publication Data
A catalog record for this book has been requested

ISBN: 978-1-138-48459-7 (hbk)
ISBN: 978-1-03-217766-3 (pbk)
DOI: 10.4324/9781351051668

Typeset in Sabon
by Apex CoVantage, LLC

Contents

To Jim and Elizabeth. You built an invulnerable fortress.

Acknowledgements

The philosophers Gilles Deleuze and Félix Guattari begin their *A Thousand Plateaus* by discussing the process of writing their previous book, *Anti-Oedipus*, together. They note (in Brian Massumi's translation): "Since each of us was several, there was already quite a crowd." If co-authorship between two people is a crowd, then how can we qualify the present book, which involved twenty-seven different people, and anywhere between three and six authors per chapter? A swarm? A hive? It was, certainly, an adventure. Viewpoints and analytical traditions rubbed against each other and generated the heat that powered the writing process. The conviction that we were contributing to a unique project—looking at authority and power from interactional perspectives—shepherded a diverse group of academics through the loopholes of collaboration until we were able, together, to produce the distinctive piece of scholarship you hold in your hands (or read on your screen). We therefore address our first thanks to the authors who have contributed to this collection of chapters.

Besides the authors, many people made it possible for this project to come to fruition. We can't possibly name everyone, but you know who you are. However, we would like to specifically express our gratitude to Lise Higham, who made the first transcription of the video data that we analyze in this book.

Contributors

Helle Kryger Aggerholm is head of research at the Danish School of Media and Journalism. Her research examines the role of communicative practices in strategic processes in public and private organizations, communication within a strategy-as-practice context, organizational communication (CCO) and language as social interaction.

Birte Asmuß is an associate professor at the Department of Management at Aarhus University, Denmark. Her main research interest is in the communicative and interactional foundations of management, leadership and organizations. She has published in leading international journals such as *Discourse Studies* and *Journal of Communication Management*.

Mariaelena Bartesaghi is an associate professor of communication at the University of Southern Florida. She studies institutionalization as dynamic between authority and accountability and by way of a synthetic and reflexive approach to discourse analysis.

Chantal Benoit-Barné is an associate professor in the Department of Communication at the Université de Montréal in Canada. Her research draws on rhetorical theories and communication as constitutive of organization (CCO) perspectives to explore the constitutive dimensions of communication in work interactions, public deliberations and sociotechnical controversies.

Geneviève Boivin is an assistant professor at the Université de Sherbrooke, Canada. Her research interests include the communicative constitution of organizations, institutional theory, intercultural communication and expatriation. Her work on the establishment of CCO scholarship has recently been published in *Management Communication Quarterly*.

Alaric Bourgoin is an assistant professor in the Department of Management at HEC Montréal, Canada. His research focuses on management consulting, value and power. Specifically, he studies the valuation practices of business consultants through a pragmatist lens. His co-authored *Capitalization: A Cultural Guide* is an anthropological investigation of the culture of contemporary capitalism.

Richard Buttny is professor of communication and rhetorical studies at Syracuse University, New York. His areas of interest include social accounting, metadiscourse and environmental discourse such as controversy on hydrofracking, animal rights or climate change.

Theresa Castor is a professor of communication at the University of Wisconsin–Parkside. Her research is in the general areas of organizational communication, and language and social interaction. Her current research involves the analysis of how risk and organizational crises are discursively constructed and the intersections of discourse, materiality and agency, with specific attention to projecting/anticipating future risks.

Huey-Rong Chen is an associate professor in the Department of Journalism, Chinese Culture University, Taiwan. As a trained researcher in Greimasian semio-narrative theory, she has applied Greimas's concepts in exploring global/local interaction/construction of identity and the relationship between technologies and human reflexivity.

Vincent Denault is a PhD candidate and lecturer at the Department of Communication of the Université de Montréal. He is the co-founder and co-director of the Center for Studies in Nonverbal Communication Sciences of the Research Center of the Montreal Mental Health University Institute.

Bertrand Fauré is an associate professor of organizational communication at the University of Toulouse. His research on the performativity of the language of numbers in organizations is published in major journals of communication and management.

Klaus Krippendorff, professor of communication at the University of Pennsylvania, addresses theories of communication, cybernetics, content analysis and design. He writes of discursive constructions of scientific, social, technological and material realities and possibilities of emancipation from burdensome social or political constructions.

Oren Livio is a lecturer at the Department of Communication, University of Haifa. His research focuses on discursive and cultural negotiations of national identity, militarism, civic participation and protest, particularly in the Israeli context.

Sky Marsen is an associate professor at Flinders University, South Australia. As a linguist and communication specialist, her interests include discourse analysis of professional writing, organizational communication and crisis communication. She has lectured at universities internationally, including at California Institute of Technology, Victoria University of Wellington and University of Southern California.

Thomas Martine is an assistant professor at Audencia Business School in Nantes, France. His research focuses on the processes of group creativity and collaborative technology in organizations. His work has been published, among others, in *Management Communication Quarterly* and *the Journal of Creative Behavior*.

Trudy Milburn is assistant dean of liberal arts & sciences at Purchase College, SUNY. She is co-editor of *Engaging and Transforming Global Communication Through Cultural Discourse Analysis* (2019) and editor of *Communicating User Experience* (2015). Her work examines discursive ways membership categories are enacted and displayed in organizational settings, both online and face-to-face.

Katherine R. Peters completed her PhD in communication at the University of Colorado–Boulder. Her research uses ethnography to investigate organizational meetings as emergent events that produce the effects of organization and culture. She is also interested in how technologies participate in communication events, like meetings, and the appearances of order and disorder in organizing.

Pierrich Plusquellec is an ethologist and associate professor in the School of Psychoeducation at the Université de Montréal, where he co-directs the Centre for Studies on Human Stress. He also co-directs the Center for Studies in Nonverbal Communication Sciences of the Research Center of the Montreal Mental Health University Institute. His publications discuss nonverbal sensitivity in relation to burnout and stress.

Jessica S. Robles is a member of the Discourse and Rhetoric Group (DARG) at Loughborough University. Her research uses discourse and conversation analysis to examine the social organization of difference and its relevance to how people interactionally manage ordinary moral troubles in their everyday lives.

Jean A. Saludadez is a professor and faculty administrator at the University of the Philippines Open University, where she also teaches communication theory and research and organizational communication at the graduate level. Her research interest is in understanding virtual organizations.

Christian Schwägerl is professor of communication management at Hochschule Osnabrück, University of Applied Sciences, Germany. He specializes in organizational communication and linguistic varieties in workplace communication.

Alena L. Vasilyeva is an assistant professor of communication at University of Massachusetts Amherst. Her general research interests include deliberation, disagreement management, social identity, communication design and the coordination of actions in personal and public contexts.

Nan Wang is an associate professor at the School of Public Administration, Hunan University. Nan completed her PhD in sociology at University of California, Los Angeles. Her research focuses on talk and social institutions. She is actively collaborating in the context of several disciplines such as communication, medicine and artificial intelligence.

Yue Yang is a PhD candidate at the University of Southern California, where she studies media and social change in China by examining how medical institutions are changing as Chinese medical professionals actively participate in online communication during China's tension-ridden healthcare reform. Her research concerns new media, controversies, contentious politics and governance of medicine in China.

Introduction

In Search for the Specific Unfolding of Authority and Power

Nicolas Bencherki, François Cooren, and Frédérik Matte

This book takes as a starting point a polemical assertion: that current literature on authority and power does not, in fact, specifically observe authority or power. This is not to say that the literature is wrong. Existing perspectives are quite correct when they provide insight on the way income, gender or racial differences are perpetuated (e.g., Ashcraft & Mumby, 2004; Lee Ashcraft & Allen, 2003) or how our views of management are rooted in war (Banerjee, 2008). These studies have drawn attention to the fact that the current state of relations between groups of people is anything but "normal," as in fact a lot of political work is involved in making them appear natural to begin with and to maintain their matter-of-fact character (Deetz, 1992).

In this sense, studies of power and authority—and related concepts—have drawn attention to the way cultural industries may obfuscate individual agency and reason (Gramsci, 1971; Horkheimer & Adorno, 2002; Kracauer, 1930, 1998), to the way documents, records, and archives are forms of population control (About & Denis, 2010; Derrida, 1996; Vismann, 2008), or to how bodies are turned into citizens through inclusion in the political body (Agamben, 1998). Authors from a range of disciplines have shown that authority and power are diffuse and shift shape to espouse the contours of the many instruments and apparatuses through which people's behavior is directed and corrected (Foucault, 1977/1995). So far, scholarship has therefore offered us a *political perspective* to our social life. To them, authority and power are vantage points from which to study society, but the notions have been deemed both too polymorphous and too fleeting to be pinned down. It has always appeared that any one definition would blind us to other centers of power and leave us vulnerable to ceaselessly renewed arrangements of control and exploitation.

Those authors who did venture definitions of power and authority have often done so by contrasting them from each other or from other neighboring notions. The first to do so was arguably Weber (1922/1968, p. 941), for whom "domination" is the "quite general" term that designates "the possibility of imposing one's own will upon the behavior of other persons," which can take the form of economic power whereby someone commands resources that correspond to the recipient's interests, while authority would consist in the "power to command and duty to obey" derived from tradition, charisma or the law. For Simon (1947/1997, p. 180), authority rests in the suspension of choice between alternatives, thus leaving the decision to the superior, whereas influence is the assessment of arguments provided and deliberate choice between options.

In contrast, Lukes (1974/1998, p. 23) views authority as the subordinate's agreement with the content of a decision or with the process through which it is reached (and it is a form of power only if it is not, in fact, consensual), thus covering both authority and influence in Simon's (1947/1997) definition. Lukes (1974/1998, p. 31) also compares his perspective to Parsons' (1967, p. 308) view of power as a "capacity to secure the performance of binding obligations by units in a system of collective organization," which arguably covers what others would view as authority. Galbraith (1983), for his part, distinguishes between condign power (or coercion), compensatory power (based on rewards) and conditioned power (based on persuasion), which take their source either from an individual's personality, property of resources or organizational hierarchy. These many contrasting, if not opposing, definitions point to the fact that power, authority and their related notions are elusive and that there is a need to change perspectives on how we approach them.

We have given just this task to the authors who contribute to this book: we asked them to share with us their perspective on how to tangibly observe and analyze authority and power. To make sure that we were all talking about the same empirical phenomenon, we added a further constraint by asking all authors to analyze the same interaction between Kim Davis, the former county clerk of Rowan County, Kentucky, and David Moore and David Ermold, a couple seeking a marriage license after the 2015 decision by the Supreme Court of the United States to strike down all bans of same-sex unions. Despite several attempts—which the couple recorded, and to which they often invited supporters and members of the press—Davis continuously refused to provide them with a marriage license, invoking her faith as a justification for her defiance of the Supreme Court ruling. It is only after Davis was incarcerated for contempt of court that, eventually, the couple was able to obtain a license.

The particular event which we asked contributors to this book to analyze took place in 2016. The excerpt, which is available on *USA Today*'s YouTube channel as well as on David Ermold's, was largely disseminated through the media and is exceptionally rich. In particular, it involves several participants besides Davis and the couple. Moore and Ermold have several supporters and members of the press on their side (including another couple who eventually joins them in requesting a marriage license). On the other side of the counter, two other clerks remain mostly silent, while Flavis McKinney, a retiree who offers Davis moral support, is more vocal in encouraging her. As the chapters will all point out, the interactional scene is therefore much more sophisticated than usual superior–subordinate models suggest, and authority is all the more fascinating to analyze. The issue at stake—gay marriage—being a hotly debated human rights problem also makes it even more challenging to remain at the level of the interaction and resist the temptation to recourse to moral or psychological explanations, for instance. Despite this added complexity, all of the chapter contributors show that it is, indeed, possible to point at *the way authority and power are concretely achieved in interaction.*

In the following section, we present the dominant view to authority and power, which we propose to refer to as a "possessive" understanding (following Tello-Rozas, Pozzebon & Mailhot, 2015). After that, we introduce a distinction between power-over, power-to and power-with (which we borrow from Follett, 1940) that helps tease out the benefits of moving past a focus on authority and power as something people possess. We then show that some precursor work has already hinted at the value of an interactional perspective before suggesting that empirical studies are already being conducted that take the interactional dimensions of authority and power seriously. This introduction ends by presenting the different chapters of this book.

The Possessive Epistemology of Power

While attempts to define authority and power have been divergent, we can observe at least some broad tendencies in the literature. Many have described power and authority following a "possessive epistemology" (Tello-Rozas et al., 2015). Indeed, authors have been conceptualizing authority and power as something people may "have," or as the outcome of having something. Hobbes (1651/1987, Chapter X) already defined power in possessive terms: "The power of a man, to take it universally, is his present means to obtain some future apparent good." More recently, Barnes (1984, p. 180) distinguished the relation between authority and power using a possessive vocabulary: "to possess authority is to possess less than to possess power." The relationship between power and possession, indeed, is solidly anchored in Western thinking (Field, 1941; Nichols, 2017), making the owning of resources a key leverage for the exercise of power. Inheriting, among others, from Locke (1689/1821; see also Keyes, 1981 on Marx), we continue to believe power derives from property (of labor, of capital, etc.), and ultimately from one's ownership of one's own self, granted by none other than God.

Among these resources, the most commonly discussed is one's hierarchical position. "Holding" a position means having "the authority to give the commands required for the discharge of these duties" (Weber, 1922/1968, p. 956). Giddens (1984, p. 258) proposes that authoritative resources derive "from the capability of harnessing the activities of human beings." Haugaard (1997, p. 111) further explains that "the actors who possess authoritative resources are those who can influence the life chances of others and/or patterns of structural reproduction." Holding that position may be achieved through bureaucratic rules but also through economic and legal tools; indeed, as Aghion and Tirole (1997, p. 2) explain, the "right to decide" is allocated through an "explicit or implicit contract," especially when it comes to shareholders' power. Power also derives from the possession of natural and technological resources. For instance, Mitchell (2013) describes how energy-production technology, in particular the switch from coal transportation by ship to oil transportation through pipelines, changes relationships of power by taking away resources from workers, including the ability to obstruct transportation activities.

Other resources whose possession grants authority and power are French and Raven's (1959) five "bases" of power—reward, coercion, legitimacy, reference and expertise. For French and Raven, these operate principally at a psychological level. For instance, reference provides a person with power over another person because the latter is attracted to or identifies with the former. Similarly, French and Raven conceive of expertise as the *perception* the recipient has of the emitter's knowledge. Social psychology has also suggested that the possession of specific skills or personality traits contributes to leadership and authority, such as different forms of intelligence in leaders (Boyatzis, Good, & Massa, 2012) or neuroticism in followers (Hetland, Sandal, & Johnsen, 2008). Each time, there is a supposition that a person—either the emitter or recipient of authority and power—may either have those sources or personality traits, or acquire them, for instance through training.

Speaking of power and authority in possessive terms can be problematic for many reasons, not the least of which being that it displaces the problem from the proprietor to the things possessed: saying that someone is powerful because they possess a resource raises the question of how that resource "has" power in its turn. For instance, how legitimacy may be "had" and how it affords authority is itself a conundrum (e.g. Ashforth & Gibbs, 1990; Erkama & Vaara, 2010). Expertise also constitutes a field of study in its own right (see Eyal, 2013). As for personality traits, the way they translate into concrete (inter)action remains problematic (see van Vuuren & Cooren, 2010).

From Having "Power-Over" to Doing "Power-With"

Instead of looking at power and authority from the perspective of the resources that would enable them, they can also be studied from the vantage point of their "uses," a perspective to which Simon (1947/1997, p. 186) hinted. For him, authority (and power, arguably) "enforces responsibility" (by allowing the imposition of sanctions on disobeying subordinates), "secures expertise in the making of decisions" (by restricting decisions to those authorized to make them) and "permits coordination of activities" (by ensuring that all subordinates follow the same general plan). These three "uses" can usefully be reworded using Follett's (1940, p. 78) distinction between power-over, power-to and power-with.

A lot of ink has been expended on the power-over perspective, which attempts to understand how an elite group of people can control others or a set of resources. This corresponds, for instance, to Dahl's (1957, p. 202) widely accepted definition: "A has power over B to the extent that he can get B to do something that B would not otherwise do." Besides the emphasis on the possession of resources discussed above, power-over is also the view adopted by many discourse-based discussions of power. For instance, Lukes (1974/1998) notes that besides the traditional focus on decision-making, studying power also requires looking at non-decision-making power, which concerns topics that are kept outside of the realm of debate, as well as at ideological power, which reveals itself in the discrepancy between real and expressed interests.

Some of Lukes' ideas can, coarsely, be seen to align with Foucault's (1977/1995), although Lukes distinguishes himself from his predecessor. In particular, Foucault views power as consisting in discursive and embodied "regimes of truths." These make power a relationship not between the powerful and the powerless but between all individuals and a constitutive feature of subjects. Authority, for its part, would consist in power relations' preoccupation with establishing their own truth, as in the case of experts such as physicians. Gramsci (1971) offers a similar view of power as stemming from hegemonic discourse: whoever can change power relations and make them appear commonsensical gains power—but being able to resist those discursive formations is power too. More recently, and with a more attentive focus on specific strategies by which hegemonic discourse is made possible, Clegg, Courpasson, and Phillips (2006, p. 2) have suggested that power follows specific "circuits," such as the episodic circuit of interactions, which in turn constitutes a dispositional circuit of meanings that form rules to be mobilized in further episodes, and a facilitative circuit that corresponds to the technologies that are put in place and that constrain or enable further episodes. Deetz (1982, 1992), for his part, stresses the importance of communication both in enabling and in revealing the naturalization of power relations, especially through specific conversational moves serving to obscure alternatives.

Building on these ideas, but shifting the emphasis to the ability of agents to act despite established systems of relations, some authors have adopted a "power-to" perspective and suggested that power should be understood as "the probability that one actor within a social relationship will be in a position to carry out his [sic] own will despite resistance" (Weber, 1922/1968, p. 53). For Giddens (1984, p. 14), this ability to act even in the face of adversity is a fundamental component of agency: "an agent ceases to be such if he or she loses the capability to 'make a difference,' that is, to exercise some sort of power." It is also at the heart of Crozier and Friedberg's (1980) understanding of power as the margin of freedom a person retains in negotiating or resisting against the system of relations where they act. Such a view undergirds new institutional perspectives, in particular the literature on "institutional work" that proposes that people can alter the structures that constrain them (Lawrence & Suddaby, 2006; Zundel, Holt, & Cornelissen, 2013).

Rather than opposing a top-down or bottom-up view of power and prioritizing either component of the "duality of structure" (Giddens, 1984, p. 15), some authors have privileged a more immanent perspective. Adopting a "power-with" approach, they have insisted on the fact that power never leaves the firm ground of relations between individuals. Hegemonic discourse, for instance, may exist, but it exists not above but between individuals. At once refuting a possessive epistemology of power and a "power-over" perspective, Arendt (1972/2001, p. 44) explains that:

> Power corresponds to the human ability not just to act but to act in concert. Power is never the property of an individual; it belongs to a group and remains in existence only so long as the group keeps together. When we say of somebody that he is "in power" we actually refer to his [sic] being empowered by a certain number of people to act in their name.

A power-with perspective, and its contrast with a possessive epistemology, is also summarized in Latour's (1986, p. 264) suggestion that power is always mediated by others: "when you simply have power— *in potentia*—nothing happens and you are powerless; when you exert power—*in actu*—others are performing the action and not you."

A Situational View of Authority

The best formulation of the power-with perspective comes from Follett (1940), who promulgated the "law of the situation," meaning that one person does not give orders to another but rather that both agree to defer to what the situation dictates. This casts the work of the researcher, but also the manager's, in a new light:

> Our job is not how to get people to obey orders, but how to devise methods by which we can best discover the order integral to a particular situation. When that is found, the employee can issue it to the employer, as well as employer to employee.
>
> (Follett, 1940, p. 35)

For Follett (1940, p. 83), the law of the situation has normative and emancipatory force: "If both sides obey the law of the situation, no person has power over another." Rather, people alter their relationships within each situation as they respond to it, thus continuously shaping new situations that "demand" new comportment from them. Follett calls for superiors and subordinates to come to a common understanding of the situation where they find themselves and to act together according to the situation's contingencies, rather than to confront each other. However, the law of the situation can also be understood as an empirical state of facts: it is the case, indeed, that people respond to continuously emerging situations, even when that situation consists in their superior giving them direct orders. The role of the researcher is to document how participants to a situation jointly figure out what it demands, how to react to it and possibly how to shape it in their turn (Bencherki & Bourgoin, in press).

A power-with perspective thus invites looking at authority and power as a situational accomplishment. This contrasts with the tendency to deductively and *a priori* define authority and power or to conflate having a clear understanding of these phenomena and reducing them to a few characteristics. A situational view, on the contrary, embraces the multifaceted, ephemeral and pervasive nature of authority, and yet paves the way to a detailed description of its inner workings. Following that path, we could hope to make power and authority accessible, at once to be researched, to be exercised and to be resisted.

Some authors have laid groundwork for a situational view of power and authority. They stress the role of communication and situate authority and power in the realm of interaction, at least in broad strokes. For instance, for Chester Barnard (1938/1968, p. 163):

> Authority is the character of a communication (order) in a formal organization by virtue of which it is accepted by a contributor to or a "member" of the organization as governing the action he contributes; that is as governing or determining what he does or is not to do so far as the organization is concerned.

While it may be read as an invitation to study what "character" in a communication makes it authoritative, thus putting the emphasis on the "message," Barnard's suggestion can also be read, in a more generous manner, as leaving room for the "recipient" of authority to choose or not to be guided by that message, thus offering elements of an interactional approach (for a comparison of studies of "message" and studies of interaction, see Pomerantz, Sanders, & Bencherki, 2018).

Herbert Simon (1947/1997, p. 178) also hints at the interactional nature of authority when he explains that "each of the coordinated individuals sets for himself a criterion of choice that makes his [sic] own behavior dependent upon the behavior of others" and that "he makes his own decision at each point as to what those adjustments should be." For Simon, authority is a "relationship" between two individuals where a superior "frames and transmits decisions with the expectation that they will be accepted by the subordinate," and where the subordinate "expects such decisions" and accepts to adjust his or her conduct to them (p. 179). While Simon can hardly be considered an analyst of interactions, he had the merit of recognizing that authority does not reside (only) in an individual's resources or skills but (also) in the relationship between people, in the expectations they hold towards each other and in the way they adjust their respective conduct according to those expectations.

However, a truly situational view of authority, living up to the program laid out by Follett and integrating the insights Barnard and Simon point out—that people orient to each other's (communicative) actions—is just beginning to be formulated. This is particularly true in the efforts of interaction scholars.

Studying Power and Authority in Interaction

Looking at authority and power from an interactional standpoint has often been deemed impossible. In particular, studies on language and social interaction have often been criticized for their alleged incapacity to deal with questions of power, coercion and domination (Cooren, 2007). By exclusively focusing on what people do in interactional scenes, these studies have indeed been accused of being ill-equipped to address and analyze what makes the interactions they study possible in the first place (Reed, 2010). They overlook, the argument goes, the key role that structures, ideologies and power relationships play in the constitution of interactions. However, it remains unclear how these structures, ideologies and power relationships concretely manifest themselves in interaction. For the past twenty years, a growing movement of scholars has decided to go beyond the sterile opposition between agency and structure by openly analyzing everything that happens to make a difference in a given interaction (Bartesaghi, 2009, 2014; Bencherki & Cooren, 2011; Benoit-Barné & Cooren, 2009; Castor & Cooren, 2006; Chiang, 2015; Cooren & Matte, 2010; Taylor & Van Every, 2011, 2014). Instead of exclusively focusing on what people do, these scholars have also considered other forms of agency or authorship that seem to make a difference through people's turns of talk.

Critical discourse analysis is probably the approach that most explicitly formulates the agenda of studying power through its manifestations in communication and interaction (Fairclough & Wodak, 1997). While it also recognizes that domination is jointly produced by the dominated, who may naturalize the uneven properties of the relationship, CDA is, however, often biased towards the study of how elites discursively reproduce their dominant position: "CDA should deal primarily with the discourse dimensions of power abuse and the injustice and inequality that result from it" (van Dijk, 1993, p. 252). CDA, in that sense, adopts a realist social ontology (Bartesaghi & Pantelides, 2018) and borrows from Marx and the Frankfurt School in an attempt to integrate the structural conditions that affect discourse and language, and the constitutive role of language in reproducing structures (van Dijk, 1993). For instance, CDA research will explore the implications of news reports using the passive voice in creating ambiguity over the source of agency (Blommaert & Bulcaen, 2000).

CDA's attempt to combine the minutiae of language with the broader context of its use has therefore brought criticism from both sides. As Bartesaghi and Pantelides (2018) point out, CDA has been accused both of adopting too narrow a perspective, thus blinding itself to the social and structural aspects of power, and, on the other side, of bringing ideological *a priori* into its analysis of discourse. In that sense, CDA is exemplar of the very dilemma confronting interaction scholars in the study of power and authority, as to whether these can be found within interaction or are to be observed outside of it.

Strictly interaction-based approaches to authority and power, which would bracket out from the analysis everything that takes place outside from the situation at hand, remain rare. Many studies have touched upon situations where relations could arguably be described as asymmetrical. This is the case of Sanders' (1995) study of the strategic enactment of superior and subordinate role-identities. Zemel and Koschmann's (2016) work on instruction during surgical training, or Davies' (1990) analysis of agency allocation in the classroom, similarly describe how, through interaction, some people are jointly constituted as authoritative and others less so. These studies, following one version or another of conversation analysis, build on the idea that authority or power do not lie in the hands of one person or another but in their interactions. This idea is strikingly obvious when looking for occurrences of the word "power" in Sacks' (1992) *Lectures on Conversation*. With few exceptions, Sacks attributes power not to people but to procedures, devices and methods that people employ as part of their interactions. The only moment when Sacks may appear to agree with the "power-over" perspective is when he attributes power to culture in his famous lecture "The baby cried. The mommy picked it up" (Sacks, 1992, p. 236). Even then, though, Sacks proceeds to discuss membership categorization devices and situates culture not in some looming, disincarnate force, but rather in people's conversational practice.

Following the idea that power pertains to interactional practices rather than to people, some rare explicit discussions of authority exist in communication studies. This is the case, for instance, of Benoit-Barné and Cooren's (2009) proposal that authority is the outcome of practices by which people invoke various figures with which they share their actions (see also Benoit-Barné & Fox, 2017). Similarly, Taylor and Van Every (2014) have shown that organizational members discursively constitute their organization as a "third" to which they agree to defer. These studies explicitly or implicitly build on Follett's (1940) view that people take their orders from the situation rather than from each other. For instance, Sanders and Bonito (2010) have shown how invoking the interest of the court proceeding or that of the judicial system in general is a way for a juror to exert influence on their peers. This sharing of the action's authorship between the juror and the institution in which they are involved thus multiplies the number of "authorities" that dictate the suggested course of action and that therefore lend it their authority.

The relationship between authority and authorship is also at play in Bartesaghi's (2009) suggestion that psychotherapist's authority proceeds from their ability to substitute patients' accounts with a therapeutic version. In agreement with this idea, other studies have shown how, in conversation, various matters of concern can come to be recognized as "co-authoring" or demanding particular courses of action, thus becoming "matters of authority." In other words, the distinction between elements that are "authoritative" and those that are not cannot be established ahead of the interactional situation where they are made relevant (Benoit-Barné & Cooren, 2009; Vásquez, Bencherki, Cooren, & Sergi, 2018).

Six Issues Concerning the Interactional Study of Authority and Power

To lay out a program for the study of authority and power from an interactional standpoint, we asked several authors—some of them well-established in the discipline, others up-and-coming—to look at the interaction between Kim Davis, David Moore and David Ermold. We asked each group of authors to ask a different question to the interaction, meaning that they had to tease out a different facet of what is going on in that county clerk's office. The analysis of a same interaction means that chapters refer to the same events, people and things. This may appear as redundant. However, as the reader will note, each approach and each chapter's focus connect those elements differently, bringing to light different relations between them. Within each chapter, we asked the different authors not to iron out their analytical differences but rather to make them apparent and to explain the merits and limitations of each interactional approach in teasing out the phenomenon being considered. Contributors, then, were honest and upfront about their different assumptions, and each guides the reader through what his or her perspective may or may not achieve to observe authority and power as they unfold in the interaction.

Chapter 1, titled "The Authority of the 'Broader Context': What's Not in the Interaction?" looks at authority by highlighting how any text is always both a product and a producer of its very context. Bartesaghi, Livio and Matte show from this "wide-angle" perspective that rapports of authority taking place locally also bring to the table broader issues situated within the larger history of intolerance and discrimination. More specifically, these authors mobilize three complementary lenses to analyse the first twenty-five lines of the interaction where a "smile" from Kim Davis brings into being a more complex storyline than what it looks like at first. Conversation analysis (CA), the notion of dislocation and critical discourse studies (CDS) are mobilized to illustrate how this apparently inoffensive smile produced by Davis makes contextually present said-to-be absentees (ideologies, past experiences, historical power structures, etc.) from other contexts. As shown in this chapter, this smile thus plays a constitutive role in the revelation of local games of authority.

While Bartesaghi, Livio and Matte demonstrate how the notion of context is first and foremost a question of definition and appropriation by actors in situations, chapter 2 addresses institutionalized and socially sanctioned forms of authority, that is, what can be considered varieties of (more or less) formal authority. Vasilyeva, Robles, Saludadez, Schwägerl and Castor show how this apparent fixed and reified authority (i.e., formal) appears, in fact, as an array of ongoing negotiations among actors throughout the interaction. These authors mobilize discourse analysis, conversation analysis and a ventriloquial approach to study authority and power as interactional accomplishment and matters of negotiation for participants in talk-in-interaction. For all of the approaches mobilized in this chapter, authority is therefore grounded in participants' actions, even if it is considered formal to begin with. Chapter 3, titled "How institutional authority and routine exertions of power can be mobilized, negotiated and challenged," invites us to study the many ways routines, rules, policies and procedures—i.e., institutionalized practices—are constitutive vectors of social encounters. Aggerholm, Asmuß, Boivin, Buttny and Krippendorff present several complementary viewpoints by which the emergence, enactment and demise of authority and power routines are analyzed. By looking at the data from a ventriloquial, accountability, micro-level as well as a multimodal routine perspective, each author of this chapter mobilizes their preferred approach to analyse the interaction. Boivin analyzes the many ways organizational actors ventriloquize and are ventriloquized by routines and procedures; Buttny discusses the role of the notion of accountability in constituting authority; Krippendorff also builds on the notion of accountability to show the critical role it plays in disrupting routine exertions of power; finally, Aggerholm and Asmuß stress the merits of multimodal analysis to look at how routines are mobilized or deviated from in constituting authority.

In chapter 4, titled "Bodies, Faces, Physical Spaces and the Materializations of Authority," we broaden the perspective about authority and power by decentering the analytical foci from human subjects. The authors of this chapter thus propose three complementary analytical positions that show how things—whether physical objects or seemingly abstract entities—fully participate in everyday interactions. Denault and

Plusquellec take insights from experimental research by comparing facial expressions to verbal statements and actions from their owner, an analysis that reveals discrepancies between the authority people invoke and what actually drives them to say what they say or do what they do. Bencherki and Bourgoin offer a transductive analysis by showing how things may participate in interaction regardless of the interpretation people make of them, as the meaning of their action proceeds for the contribution they make to broader activities. Finally, Cooren and Huey-Rong mobilize a ventriloquial perspective to show how the three people involved in the heated discussion can be positioned or position themselves as the channels by which other elements end up speaking and making a difference in the way the situation evolves.

In chapter 5, titled "God, Love and the Apparently Immaterial Sources of Authority," Fauré, Martine, Milburn and Peters envisage sources of authority that appear, at first sight, rather abstract and immaterial. These authors indeed focus their analysis on nothing other than love and God by showing how they can be brought into being through speech, tone and visible actions. To do so, they mobilize four complementary lenses to analyze how actors in the scene manage to evoke or invoke these sources of authority in their respective turns of talk. Martine uses a constitutive view of communication to show the very materialization of love and God in the interaction and the relative authority they acquire as a result. Peters presents an ethnography of communication perspective to stress the part cultural and historical understandings play a part in authority. Milburn, for her part, draws on cultural discourse analysis to show that cultural premises can be displayed or located in discursive practices and therefore that authority is manifested in the way people act and relate. Finally, Fauré looks at God and love as symmetrical authorities that can be more or less materialized, drawing attention to the notion of absence.

Last but not least, chapter 6, titled "Decentering the Analysis: The Authority of Spectators, Journalists and Others," offers yet another way to push the boundaries about authority by drawing attention to a broader range of people and objects in the scene, including those who do not speak. All four approaches mobilized in this chapter agree that authority is a dynamic and fluid phenomenon that is negotiated in social interactions even by agents that remain invisible. Benoit-Barné sees authority as being a relational occurrence happening through presentification. For Marsen, authority is mainly discursive and is manifested in the positioning of agents as well as the description of their actions and words by a narrator. For Yang, power and authority relate to widely shared assumptions by participants even if their manifestation depends largely on the situational constructions of relationships and identities. Finally, Wang mobilizes a conversation analytic approach to show how authority is socially constructed through participants' exchange of social actions.

Conclusion: Future Direction for Research

Our hope with this book is twofold. On the one hand, we want to contribute to current conversations regarding authority and power, for instance in the fields of sociology or management, by showing that it is possible to specifically point to the interactional dynamics by which these phenomena materialize in each specific situation. This is important not only as an academic exercise to offer more analytical minutiae for the study of otherwise evanescent notions but also as a political project, as we strongly believe that providing concrete leverage for either exercising or resisting authority and power can only be done when we better understand their concrete, day-to-day unfolding. Indeed, as long as we speak of these notions in abstract terms, they will continue to appear unescapable, as if authority and power were already there, surrounding and trapping us. The fact may be, though, that we surround and trap each other in a joint accomplishment that we often more or less consciously deny afterwards.

On the other hand, we also want to make authority and power salient problems within the language and social interaction community. These notions have often appeared to be too loaded to researchers who have preferred to speak in terms of "directing," "instructing," "holding accountable" and so forth. The fact, though, is that these may correspond precisely to what other social scientists refer to as authority and power, although at a different level of detail. Interaction scholars are often reluctant to address "big issues" that may appear well beyond the scope of their studies of localized interactions. Yet, they also claim that there is nothing that is not local: this means that phenomena of authority and power can never be "beyond" their reach. It is therefore up to them, also, to provide their own contribution to questions that certainly concern the members they observe.

By stating that questions of authority and power are not their concerns, some interaction scholars may paradoxically reproduce two distinctions that they claim to reject, namely the micro vs. macro distinction (by thinking that these issues are beyond their scope) and the member vs. analyst distinction (by refusing to use members' terms). It is therefore about time to reappropriate those notions to show how they constitute interactional accomplishment and, in the process, make them less taboo for us as well as for those who must deal with them in their daily life.

References

About, I., & Denis, V. (2010). *Histoire de l'identification des personnes.* Paris: La Découverte.

Agamben, G. (1998). *Homo sacer: Sovereign power and bare life.* Stanford, CA: Stanford University Press.

Aghion, P., & Tirole, J. (1997). Formal and real authority in organizations. *Journal of Political Economy, 105*(1), 1–29. https://doi.org/10.2307/2138869

Arendt, H. (2001). *On violence* (1st edition). New York, NY: Mariner Books. (Original work published 1972).

Ashcraft, K. L., & Mumby, D. K. (2004). *Reworking gender: A feminist communicology of organization.* Thousand Oaks, CA: Sage. Retrieved from www.loc. gov/catdir/toc/ecip046/2003016116.html

Ashforth, B. E., & Gibbs, B. W. (1990). The double-edge of organizational legitimation. *Organization Science, 1*(2), 177–194. https://doi.org/10.1287/orsc.1.2.177

Banerjee, S. B. (2008). Necrocapitalism. *Organization Studies, 29*(12), 1541–1563. https://doi.org/10.1177/0170840607096386

Barnard, C. (1968). *The functions of the executive.* Cambridge: Harvard University Press. (Original work published 1938).

Barnes, B. (1984). On authority and its relationship to power. *The Sociological Review, 32*, 180–195. https://doi.org/10.1111/j.1467-954X.1984.tb00112.x

Bartesaghi, M. (2009). How the therapist does authority: Six strategies for substituting client accounts in the session. *Communication & Medicine, 6*(1), 15–25.

Bartesaghi, M. (2014). Coordination: Examining weather as a "matter of concern". *Communication Studies, 65*(5), 535–557. https://doi.org/10.1080/1051 0974.2014.957337

Bartesaghi, M., & Pantelides, K. (2018). Why critique should not run out of steam: A proposal for the critical study of discourse. *Review of Communication, 18*(3), 158–177.

Bencherki, N., & Bourgoin, A. (in press). "And who are you again?": A performative perspective on authority in organizations. *Academy of Management Journal.*

Bencherki, N., & Cooren, F. (2011). Having to be: The possessive constitution of organization. *Human Relations, 64*(12), 1579–1607. https://doi.org/10.1177/0018726711424227

Benoit-Barné, C., & Cooren, F. (2009). The accomplishment of authority through presentification: How authority is distributed among and negotiated by organizational members. *Management Communication Quarterly, 23*(1), 5–31. https://doi.org/10.1177/0893318909335414

Benoit-Barné, C., & Fox, S. (2017). Authority. In *The international encyclopedia of organizational communication.* Hoboken, NJ: John Wiley & Sons, Inc. https://doi.org/10.1002/9781118955567.wbieoc011

Blommaert, J., & Bulcaen, C. (2000). Critical discourse analysis. *Annual Review of Anthropology, 29*(1), 447–466. https://doi.org/10.1146/annurev.anthro.29.1.447

Boyatzis, R. E., Good, D., & Massa, R. (2012). Emotional, social, and cognitive intelligence and personality as predictors of sales leadership performance. *Journal of Leadership & Organizational Studies, 19*(2), 191–201. https://doi. org/10.1177/1548051811435793

Castor, T., & Cooren, F. (2006). Organizations as hybrid forms of life: The implications of the selection of agency in problem formulation. *Management Communication Quarterly, 19*(4), 570–600. https://doi.org/10.1177/0893318905284764

Chiang, S.-Y. (2015). Power and discourse. In K. Tracy, C. Ilie, & T. Sandel (Eds.), *The international encyclopedia of language and social interaction.* Hoboken, NJ: John Wiley & Sons, Inc. Retrieved from http://onlinelibrary.wiley.com/doi/10.1002/9781118611463.wbielsi149/abstract

Clegg, S. R., Courpasson, D., & Phillips, N. (2006). *Power and organizations*. Thousand Oaks, CA: Sage.

Cooren, F. (Ed.). (2007). *Interacting and organizing: Analyses of a management meeting*. Mahwah, NJ: Lawrence Erlbaum Associates, Publishers.

Cooren, F., & Matte, F. (2010). For a constitutive pragmatics: Obama, Médecins Sans Frontières and the measuring stick. *Pragmatics and Society, 1*(1), 9–31. https://doi.org/10.1075/ps.1.1.02coo

Crozier, M., & Friedberg, E. (1980). *Actors and systems: The politics of collective action*. Chicago, IL: University of Chicago Press.

Dahl, R. A. (1957). The concept of power. *Behavioral Science, 2*(3), 201–215.

Davies, B. (1990). Agency as a form of discursive practice. A classroom scene observed. *British Journal of Sociology of Education, 11*(3), 341–361. https://doi.org/10.2307/1392847

Deetz, S. A. (1982). Critical interpretive research in organizational communication. *Western Journal of Communication, 46*(2), 131–149.

Deetz, S. A. (1992). *Democracy in an age of corporate colonization: Developments in communication and the politics of everyday life*. Albany: State University of New York.

Derrida, J. (1996). *Archive fever: A freudian impression*. (E. Prenowitz, Trans.). Chicago: University of Chicago Press.

Erkama, N., & Vaara, E. (2010). Struggles over legitimacy in global organizational restructuring: A rhetorical perspective on legitimation strategies and dynamics in a shutdown case. *Organization Studies, 31*(7), 813–839. https://doi.org/10.1177/0170840609346924

Eyal, G. (2013). For a sociology of expertise: The social origins of the autism epidemic. *American Journal of Sociology, 118*(4), 863–907. https://doi.org/10.1086/668448

Fairclough, N., & Wodak, R. (1997). Critical discourse analysis. In T. A. van Dijk (Ed.), *Discourse as social interaction* (pp. 258–284). Thousand Oaks, CA: Sage.

Field, O. P. (1941). Property and authority. *The Journal of Politics, 3*(3), 253–275. https://doi.org/10.2307/2125564

Follett, M. P. (1940). *The dynamic administration: The collected papers of Mary Parker Follett*. London: Routledge.

Foucault, M. (1995). *Discipline and punish: The birth of the prison*. New York: Vintage Books. (Original work published 1977).

French, J. R. P., & Raven, B. (1959). The bases of social power. In D. Cartwright (Ed.), *Studies in social power* (pp. 150–167). Oxford: University of Michigan Press.

Galbraith, J. K. (1983). *The anatomy of power*. Boston, MA: Houghton Mifflin.

Giddens, A. (1984). *The constitution of society: Outline of the theory of structuration*. Cambridge, UK: Polity Press.

Gramsci, A. (1971). *Selections from the prison notebooks*. (Q. Hoare & G. Nowell Smith, Trans.). New York, NY: International.

Haugaard, M. (1997). *The constitution of power: A theoretical analysis of power, knowledge and structure*. Manchester: Manchester University Press.

Hetland, H., Sandal, G. M., & Johnsen, T. B. (2008). Followers' personality and leadership. *Journal of Leadership & Organizational Studies, 14*(4), 322–331. https://doi.org/10.1177/1548051808315550

Hobbes, T. (1987). *Leviathan*. London: Dent. (Original work published 1651).

Horkheimer, M., & Adorno, T. W. (2002). *Dialectic of enlightenment*. (G. Schmid Noerr, Ed., E. Jephcott, Trans.). Stanford, CA: Stanford University Press.

Keyes, T. W. (1981). *Karl marx on property* (Ph.D.). Marquette University, Milwaukee, WI. Retrieved from http://search.proquest.com/docview/303183896/abstract

Kracauer, S. (1998). *The salaried masses: Duty and distraction in Weimar Germany*. (Q. Hoare, Trans.). London: Verso. (Original work published 1930).

Latour, B. (1986). The powers of association. In J. Law (Ed.), *Power, action and belief: A new sociology of knowledge?* (pp. 264–280). London: Routledge.

Lawrence, T. B., & Suddaby, R. (2006). Institution and institutional work. In S. R. Clegg, C. Hardy, T. B. Lawrence, & W. R. Nord (Eds.), *Sage handbook of organization studies* (2nd edition, pp. 215–254). Thousand Oaks, CA: Sage.

Lee Ashcraft, K., & Allen, B. J. (2003). The racial foundation of organizational communication. *Communication Theory, 13*(1), 5–38. https://doi.org/10.1111/j.1468-2885.2003.tb00280.x

Locke, J. (1821). *Two treatises of government*. London: Whitmore Fenn, and C. Brown. (Original work published 1689).

Lukes, S. (1998). *Power: A radical view* (Reprint). Houndmills: Macmillan. (Original work published 1974).

Mitchell, T. (2013). *Carbon democracy: Political power in the age of oil* (2nd Revised edition). London: Verso.

Nichols, R. (2017). Theft is property! The recursive logic of dispossession. *Political Theory*. https://doi.org/10.1177/0090591717701709

Parsons, T. (1967). *Sociological theory and modern society*. New York: Free Press.

Pomerantz, A., Sanders, R. E., & Bencherki, N. (2018). Communication as the study of social action: On the study of language and social interaction: An interview with Anita Pomerantz and Robert E. Sanders, by Nicolas Bencherki. *Communiquer. Revue de Communication Sociale et Publique, 22*, 103–118.

Reed, M. (2010). Is communication constitutive of organization? *Management Communication Quarterly, 24*(1), 151–157. https://doi.org/10.1177/0893318909351583

Sacks, H. (1992). *Lectures on conversation*. (G. Jefferson, Ed.). Cambridge, MA: Blackwell.

Sanders, R. E. (1995). A neo-rhetorical perspective: The enactment of role-identities as interactive and strategic. In S. J. Sigman (Ed.), *The consequentiality of communication* (pp. 67–120). Hillsdale, NJ: Erlbaum.

Sanders, R. E., & Bonito, J. A. (2010). Speaking for the institution: A fourth production site for group members' influence attempts. *Small Group Research, 41*(4), 427–451. https://doi.org/10.1177/1046496410366309

Simon, H. A. (1997). *Administrative behavior: A study of decision-making processes in administrative organizations* (4th edition). New York: Free Press. (Original work published 1947).

Taylor, J. R., & Van Every, E. J. (2011). *The situated organization: Studies in the pragmatics of communication research*. New York, NY: Routledge.

Taylor, J. R., & Van Every, E. J. (2014). *When organization fails: Why authority matters*. New York, NY: Routledge.

Tello-Rozas, S., Pozzebon, M., & Mailhot, C. (2015). Uncovering micro-practices and pathways of engagement that scale up social-driven collaborations: A practice view of power: Micro-practices and pathways of engagement. *Journal of Management Studies*, n/a–n/a. https://doi.org/10.1111/joms.12148

van Dijk, T. A. (1993). Principles of critical discourse analysis. *Discourse & Society*, *4*(2), 249–283. https://doi.org/10.1177/0957926593004002006

van Vuuren, M., & Cooren, F. (2010). "My attitude made me do it": Considering the agency of attitudes. *Human Studies*, *33*(1), 85–101. https://doi.org/10.1007/s10746-010-9137-x

Vásquez, C., Bencherki, N., Cooren, F., & Sergi, V. (2018). From "matters of concern" to "matters of authority": Reflecting on the performativity of strategy in writing a strategic plan. *Long-Range Planning*, *51*(3), 417–435. https://doi.org/10.1016/j.lrp.2017.01.001

Vismann, C. (2008). *Files: Law and media technology*. (G. Winthrop-Young, Trans.). Stanford, CA: Stanford University Press.

Weber, M. (1968). *Economy and society: An outline of interpretive sociology*. New York, NY: Bedminster Press. (Original work published 1922).

Zemel, A., & Koschmann, T. (2016). A stitch in time: Instructing temporality in the operating room. *Communication & Medicine*, *12*(1), 85–98. https://doi.org/10.1558/cam.v12i1.25988

Zundel, M., Holt, R., & Cornelissen, J. (2013). Institutional work in the wire an ethological investigation of flexibility in organizational adaptation. *Journal of Management Inquiry*, *22*(1), 102–120. https://doi.org/10.1177/1056492612440045

1 The Authority of the "Broader Context"

What's Not in the Interaction?

*Mariaelena Bartesaghi, Oren Livio,
and Frédérik Matte*

In a recent volume devoted to exploring the notion of context, Flowerdew (2014) notes that discourse analysis (DA):

> is concerned with the interpretation of texts and (. . .) how texts are related to the contexts in which they are produced and received. An understanding of context is thus an essential feature of the analysis. [Though] (. . .) discourse analysis has spent a lot of time identifying the structure and functions which make up text and talk (. . .) there has been relatively less emphasis on defining *just what is meant by context*.
>
> (p. 2, our emphasis)

By inviting us to take up a context that is not—and yet is presumed to be—authoritatively *there*, this chapter engages us in a prima facie paradox: how are we to define what is *not* unless we know what *is*?

According to the Merriam-Webster Dictionary, a context consists of: "1) the parts of a discourse that surround a word or passage and can throw light on its meaning; 2) the interrelated conditions in which something exists or occurs: environment, setting" ("Context," 2019). Hence the granular conundrum of context, a notion so deeply ingrained in our understanding about communication as to be deemed unproblematic. On the one hand, a context is anything that can be considered *present*—people's bodies, spoken and written discourse, and artefacts, as well as what is supposedly *absent*, non-apparent, implicit, or transient—such as ideologies, cultural background, or past experiences. It is "what [a discourse analyst] need[s] to know in order to properly understand the event, [inter] action or discourse" (van Dijk, 1977, p. 11). On the other hand, the very ambiguity of the term presents an *et cetera problem* (c.f. Garfinkel, 1967) for discourse analysis where context is a fill-in-the-blanks prescription: from a container for interaction (Schegloff, 1997) to "a variable among other variables (. . .) in the explanatory equation" (Buttny, 1993, p. 161). Thus, for analysts to define context (more or less broadly) is to claim what it is we are doing when we do DA.

In what follows, we take preliminary steps to address how context appears to authorize texts, positioning us as authors of our own analyses. We first situate the interaction between Kim Davis, David Moore, and David Ermold by capturing three instances of contextual intelligibility for DA: the conversation analysis (CA)-DA debate, the notion of dislocation, and the broader framework offered by critical discourse studies (CDS). Next, we suggest our own analyses to illustrate and realize these definitions. We conclude by discussing the value and challenges involved in "analyzing one text from [different] perspectives" (Stubbe et al., 2003, p. 380) and by examining how choices about contexts exercise authority over our analysis of an interaction and, in fact, reveal and conceal the situation itself.

Mobilizing Contexts

In spite of methodological disagreements, different approaches to discourse analysis do share fundamental orientations. We all consider social identities as active interactional accomplishments, see them as mobilized in orderly and sequential fashion, and examine them as situated in social and historical practices that re-create the universe we inhabit (Korobov, 2001). How context comes into play is another matter altogether. Critical discourse analysis (CDA) has been accused of fuzziness (Flowerdew, 2014) and sometimes of downright failure in making good on its claim of examining text and context dialectically (see Blommaert, 2005). At the same time, CA has been attacked as being ideologically disingenuous in its claims regarding situated and endogenous orientations to context by interactional participants (Billig, 1999).

Such cross-denunciations, which reached their zenith in the ongoing page-turner between CA representative Emanuel Schegloff and multiple authors speaking for (C)DA in the pages of *Discourse & Society*,[1] arise because the notion of context, in and of itself, indexes and legitimates a metadiscourse of allegiances and belonging (see Tracy, 1998). The epistemic battle between CA and DA[2] has to do with the former approach's attempt to define the territory of conversation as both context independent and context sensitive, that is, endemic to social life as well as locally managed. Conversation analysts thus claim to "*reveal* how participants' own interpretations of the ongoing exchange inform their conduct" (Wooffitt, 2005, p. 86, our emphasis). Laying no such claim, DA is accused of falling back on analyst presuppositions (e.g., Antaki, Billig, Edwards, & Potter, 2003; Wooffitt, 2005).

CA's analytical warrant is worth looking into. Take the very interaction we are analyzing, which initially bore the title "Watch Kentucky clerk defy Supreme Court on gay marriage" (2015). This suggests that the clerk's defiance occurs in the immediate interaction; and yet there are no Supreme Court judges speaking. Rather, the reference to the Supreme

Court and to gay marriage is an instruction regarding how to engage with the speakers present, as well as how to locate and trace the voices of those supposedly absent. So, the title serves as a context by an analyst and for an analyst to understand the interaction as part of a broader intertextual picture.

Now let us remove the title and focus "only" on the interactants' situated context-making, as CA would have it. Is the transcript of the interaction and/or the video the text itself? To take this position would illustrate what Billig (1999, p. 573) calls "naïve epistemology and methodology." CA notions of interactional machineries and simple systematics notwithstanding, choices as to how talk is to be entextualized (including the fact that it goes from left to right, the numbering of lines, and choices as to the level of detail of notation symbols) are inevitably analyst-made theory not shared by the interactants and as such inescapably political (see Bucholz, 2000, 2007; Ochs, 1979).

A video, too, is context, for what the camera displays (Jones, 2009) of the material, incarnate, and affective universe (Iedema, 2011) interprets and orders our seeing and thus what we consider data. What interactants "orient" to—to use the CA verb par excellence—is not intrinsic to one conversation but rather an ongoing, contingent, and shifting relevance in contextual focus, or a matter of how "the world is observed, noticed, and experienced by members of a society in the range of settings in which they live their lives" (Schegloff, 2000, p. 718). With these words, Schegloff himself appears to admit that analysts count as observers. More about this will be taken up in our first analysis.

Broadening Our Query

Because of its preoccupation with the situated, CA risks missing how a conversation's threads are woven into a richer backcloth of multiply embedded contexts (c.f. Jones, 2016; Wetherell, 1998). The notion of dislocation recognizes this, for a scene, a context, or a moment is always influenced or contaminated by other traces, marks, or aspects of what could be considered outside of the (con)text but that are nonetheless evoked, convoked, or talked into being by interactants through space and time (Vásquez & Cooren, 2013). As Cooren (2010) proposes:

> There is therefore dis-location to the extent that interactions are never purely local. They are always *dislocal*, . . . that is, they constantly mobilize entities that they contribute to re-present, making them present in the here and now. Interestingly, this way of conceiving of interaction precisely allows us to free it from the *hic et nunc*, from the *present* in both senses of the term (spatial and temporal).
>
> (pp. 2–3, emphases in original)

For instance, past events, previous relationships, or prior encounters might be addressed in a conversation to anchor the subject matter or rapport between people. Someone could also invoke informal rules or tacit agreements as a way of reminding everyone in a meeting that, even if not explicitly stated, they might be making a difference in the way the situation is being shaped. Thus, all these supposedly out-of-context features can be mobilized in a conversation to enhance an argument, convince someone, or simply talk about the reminiscence of events or the possible consequences of something to come.

A dislocal perspective encourages analysts to broaden their view on what a particular context implies and the opportunities (and limits) of studying its constitution-in-the-making. Accordingly, it is possible to better appreciate the eventful as well as the iterative features of any communicational phenomenon that, by proxy, instantiates what could be considered external social apparatuses such as hierarchal status, institutions, or beliefs (Fairhurst & Cooren, 2009). As an empirical example of dislocation, we will later focus our attention on the many authorities at play in the scene analyzed, authorities that can be envisaged as anything that potentially gives credibility, power, or reliability by providing weight or making a difference to someone's actions (Benoit-Barné & Cooren, 2009). As suggested by Cooren (2010):

> It is indeed not by chance, as Taylor and Van Every (2000) reminded us, that authority and author have the same Latin root (*auctor*), in that it means that whoever or whatever is explicitly or implicitly positioned as a *figure* of authority will also be staged as *authoring* what is asserted or put forward.
>
> (p. 108, emphases in original)

And Broadening It Still

Critical discourse analysis (CDA) attempts to link approaches to context focusing on both relatively "local" characteristics and broader features. Since CDA considers elements such as structural relations of power, dominant ideologies, and the analyst's own positioning—elements not readily identifiable within the text—as central to defining what the relevant "context" is, identifying these features is vital. Yet, in line with CDA's self-identification as a loosely organized network rather than a unified theory or method (Wodak & Meyer, 2009), different CDA approaches emphasize different components when considering context's role in analysis. We highlight three central approaches here.

Van Dijk (2008, 2009) eschews reductionist perspectives to context as a mere external social attribute related to the environment or structure in which discourse occurs (e.g., gender, age, or class). What is important for him is how these attributes are translated cognitively into an *internal* "subjective mental representation, a dynamic online model, of the participants about the for-them-now relative properties of the communicative situation" (van Dijk, 2009, p. 66). Van Dijk refers to such representations as "context models": pragmatic, subjective, and dynamic definitions made by participants regarding what is relevant in a given situation. It is not any inherent characteristic of the situation that determines how discourse is produced but rather how participants perceive and represent these characteristics mentally and render them relevant (van Dijk, 2008, pp. 164–169). Context models are always dynamic and realized through schemas made up of categories such as spatial and temporal settings; participants and their roles, goals, and ideologies; and various forms of knowledge (van Dijk, 2009). As we will see in the last of our analyses, differences in their context models may help explain conflicts between participants.

Fairclough (e.g., 1992) considers context as both local-verbal (the preceding and following texts) and external-situational (i.e., the relevant characteristics of the social situation in which texts occur). These contexts are shaped differently in different discursive formations or types of discourse associated with specific rules, norms, and practices (e.g., medicine or law). Combining these insights, Fairclough (1992) examines context on three interrelated levels: (1) the immediate textual context, or how the text is shaped by what comes before and after it; (2) the context of discursive practice, or the processes of production, distribution, and consumption that are associated with a specific type of discourse; and (3) the context of social practice, or broader social conditions in which ideology and power play a central role. Fairclough's approach thus requires attention to all three levels of context simultaneously, as each reflects, shapes, and constrains the workings of the other two.

Wodak's Discourse-Historical Approach (DHA) focuses more explicitly on the historical context, which may refer alternatively to the relatively brief time scales of a specific event or to larger scale changes over time (Wodak, 2014). Analytically, DHA offers a four-level heuristic model which includes: (1) the immediate textual surroundings—much like Fairclough; (2) other texts and discourses that the text relates to explicitly or implicitly; (3) extralinguistic social, environmental, and situational elements, usually based upon ethnographic observation; and (4) broader sociopolitical and historical conditions in which the discourse is embedded (Wodak, 2011, 2014).

Three Contexts and a Smile

For the approaches we have briefly surveyed, determining what context should be called upon to authorize an interaction is not merely a methodological issue but rather theoretical and consequential to what the analysis materializes as being *the* situation. We now turn to examine how this operates in practice through three successive analyses of the interaction in question.

Reading Smiles

Mariaelena Bartesaghi

In our opening analysis, we ask: how is context a (morally) account-able (c.f. Garfinkel, 1967) order between interactants and text? By considering how speakers mobilize context as an interactional resource, we also attend to the relationship between its iterability and its fluidity. By iterability, we mean that speakers are able to appropriate the text in ways that others will recognize and therefore rework; by fluidity, we mean that recontextualizations allow for speakers to shift positions both within a recognized context and an unfolding text, making context anew. As very much a participant in this moral tension and unfolding, we invite the analyst to account for their own authorship of context by way of an analysis or an authoritative reading of the "interaction order" (Goffman, 1983).

This is particularly so once multimodality enters the scene, offering new openings for context that may prove to trip us up if we are not careful. To illustrate our argument, we present two extracts in which a smile is a morally accountable text to interactants, contingent on the contexts of its reading(s). The first is from the exchange between Ermold, Moore, and Davis.

Extract 1

3	ERMOLD	Don't smile at [me
4	MOORE	[Here she is
5		(0.5)
6	DAVIS	I did not smile
7		(2.0)
8	DAVIS	I'm not being disrespectful to you ((shaking her head))

A great deal happens in only four turns of talk: Kim Davis (1) is declared as smiling, (2) negated the moral entitlement to smile (line 3), and (3) is declared by Moore (whose contribution overlaps Ermold's collaboratively at the point where Davis has been told not to smile) as the "she" whose presence is notable and thus worthy of an account (line 4). After a notable (line 5) pause, Davis (4) denies smiling. And (5) following an even longer pause (line 7), in which for 2.0 seconds no other speakers take their turn, Davis (6) repairs her previous turn (see Fox, 2012), recasting her actions in terms of (dis)respect. This is an implicit denial of smiling but with different moral stakes altogether. Let us turn to points 1–6 above in terms of negotiation of text and context.

With each contribution, participants formulate morally implicative accounts that demand accounts be produced in response (Buttny, 1993; Grimshaw, 1990; Robles & Castor, 2017) in the turn-by-turn construction of a shared moral "text." Davis's denial of having smiled (line 6) after a pause tells us that the smile is indeed the text in question. That is, the speakers are now aligned in the production of a text-context iteration, in which smiling or not smiling is the moral issue at hand. The adjudication of the reading of the text as smiling or not smiling will order the speakers within a different moral account. Nonetheless, each must take their conversational turn for a particular version to unfold as such. In a sense, Ermold and Moore are waiting for the situation to "come off" (as Sacks would say) according to their version of context: a situation in which Davis's smile is inappropriate and a face-threat that merits an equally face-threatening negative injunction (line 3). In sum, an iteration in which she is morally accountable as a bigot and as breaking the law for not issuing Ermold and Moore a marriage license.

But Davis does something quite eventful. Though still cooperating with the text of the smile, she reclaims it as context for the conflict; in fact she recontextualizes it within her own ongoing (by virtue of grammatical construction in line 6, "I am not being") moral stance. By affiliating with the men's version that she may have indeed been smiling (for admitting not disrespecting (line 8) is, by implication, an admission that something that could have been interpreted as such *did* happen), she reworks the shared and fluid context of present and future trouble in favor of a position in which her morality is not impugnable, and her possible smile is very much appropriate. That is, she is not disrespectful because she is right! She is defying the gay couple! Supporters are watching! God is watching! She also ironicizes and rebuts the men's moral reading and censuring of her facial expression (see Petitjean & González-Martínez, 2015).

By pursuing the initial claim that the face is the text and its uptakes are candidate moral contexts that authorize its reading, let us move to the exchange of Extract 2 (from Bartesaghi, 2015):

Extract 2

M: Mother, T: Therapist

1	T	Somebody's gonna get killed. Somebody's gonna
2		die in your house=
3	M	=It's not that VIOlent=
4	T	=I see her face this is as violent as it gets (.)
5		someone's gonna get KILLED

Though taken from different interactions in very different institutional settings, Extracts 1 and 2 nonetheless refer us to a broader context where faces are readable texts of trouble, moral accounts, and asymmetries of accounting. Both exchanges require that interactants arrange themselves with respect to a "display" (Jones, 2009, pp. 115–116). As such, a display is a text that reflexively creates the site or context in which it occurs, and the practice it organizes in this site is significant to its interpreters or "watchers" (Scollon, 1998), who are positioned as readers/analysts of the text.

We notice in Extract 2 that the mother and therapist are co-watchers but claiming very different views of the display, like Ermold, Moore, and Davis, who are engaged in ratifying candidate moral contexts for a smile. In this extract, the therapist sees the face as a display or text for a reading of violence (line 4), a dysfunctional household (line 2), and a death foretold (lines 1 and 5). The mother, who cannot step as far away as the therapist to position herself as an expert observer of the display, cannot offer what the therapist does: the dispassionate yet keen scientific (in) sight of a mental expert connecting a face to statistics of faces and death and the psychology of violent murders in dysfunctional families.

Similarly, although Davis is aware of her own display in the immediate context of the watch and the parties present, an awareness that gradually becomes manifest as the transcript continues beyond line 25, and more immediately by Ermold's uptake in line 9, it is arguable that she is the spectacle here and that the watch engages others to organize their responses in order to incite more contexts and occasions for her displays of (fill in the blank) moral inadequacy.

In sum, the idea of a watch—comprised of the spectacle *and* its watchers—is analogous to the analytical possibilities of text and context as a constantly regenerating and renewing relationship between figure and ground. With the recent multimodal turn in DA (e.g., Flowerdew, 2014; Iedema, 2011),[3] screenshots from video recordings have populated analyses, allowing us new texts and contexts of watching.[4] We now lay claim not only to what it is about a smile that is significant or "empirically viable" (Robles & Castor, 2017, p. 12) but also to whether *we* can tell if the smile is there. More troublesome (though the analyses that follow will differ in this assessment), our analyses of what interactants see/ do not see collapse the embeddedness of their watching with that of the camera.

Jones (2009) cautions us that:

> the problem with examining sites of display outside of the context of their use by "watchers" to perform particular social practices is that what people can do with different sites of display alters radically in different contexts.

> (p. 114)

The rub may lie in unreflexively moving to broader analytical contexts, perhaps not considering how, in so doing, we authorize a Goffmanian interaction order of reading faces and the readers of faces (and so on up the chain of indexicality) and texts for our own "watching" and reading, and ours alone.

Dislocation: A Smile Is More Than a Smile to Start With

Frédérik Matte

As we briefly mentioned in the beginning, a dislocal perspective allows us to see that any said-to-be local interaction is in fact a point of convergence where many "imports" from afar, beyond, and above are brought to life: past stories and experiences might be evoked or other actors shall be convoked, for instance. In this case, it appears that we are witnessing a battle of contexts, so to speak. Ermold and Moore are precisely "dislocalizing" the interaction by attempting to bring in elements of their past interactions with Davis, while she tries to "localize" it in the immediate situation, thus denying the contextualization that the men attempt to make. Of course, if the two men succeed in showing that they have past interactions, that the Supreme Court has already rendered judgment that is relevant to this situation, that this is an instance of denial of gay rights, etc. . . . Davis would clearly be "losing the battle," so to speak.

Incidentally, we can see in line 3 that Ermold bluntly tells Davis, who is just arriving at the counter from her office: "Don't smile at me." To this Davis replies straightforwardly, "I did not smile." So, what is there to say from a dislocal point of view about these two turns of talk initiating the conversation to come? First, we note that without any hesitation and using the imperative—the tone appears to be defiant, with a strong and loud pronunciation of the word "Don't"—Ermold authorizes himself to forthrightly tell Davis not to smile.

There seems to be dislocation to the extent that "Don't smile at me" is a way to react not only to Davis's smile but also to the discrepancy between their past history and the smile, which appears fake to Ermold because it contrasts with the previous encounters that are spectrally presentified through this one. We thus might infer that if someone allows themselves to begin a conversation by using such a directive and authoritative mode, there must be a past conversation or historical relation that potentially explains or justifies such a defiant attitude. Ermold seems to take the liberty to tell someone with an official and public status that this representative cannot smile, a directive and blunt utterance that appears at odds with how the relation between a constituent and a representative of the State would customarily begin.

One would not expect smiling to a constituent to be negatively sanctioned. Nevertheless, Davis does not appear to be surprised by Ermold's directive and simply replies in a somewhat plain and calm fashion—her tone of voice is very low—that she "did not smile." If we look closely at the video excerpt, however, we can see that Davis does in fact show off a minor smile, contradicting what she herself claimed she was not doing to Ermold. As analysts, it would certainly be too suggestive to insinuate that Davis is producing an ironic smile precisely to acknowledge the irony of the present situation. Nevertheless, Davis appears to smile to communicate to Ermold and Moore that she might be willing to play her institutional role on the surface—smiling at constituents for whom Davis is working does not seem unusual—but that she will most certainly stay on the surface (of her official role) and only *pretend* to help them out with their issue, in which she does not appear to believe.

In a nutshell, the discrepancy between Davis's smile, Ermold's reaction to it, and then Davis's apparent indifference to his negative reaction, suggests that the two parties have met previously in a similar setting, arguing about the same issue. Thus, if we wish to better understand how authority—and power to a lesser extent—are both at play in the first turn of talk, we must also take into account its effects of dislocation. One analytical way of doing so is to look precisely at how the discourse mobilized is never located only on the surface, so to speak, but also contains or encloses characteristics that seem to be imported or convoked by interactants—as well as being inscribed in the utterance. The authoritative tone used by Ermold to begin the conversation tells us a somehow different story than what the situation appears to be to start with; that is, it is a bit out of tone in the circumstances of a meeting with a government representative.

Davis's smile, in that sense, brings into the interaction extra-situational agencies—the previous meetings do *matter* in this situation—by showing Ermold and Moore that she is probably well aware of the demands to come. She appears to recognize that this conversation is a sequel to what has happened in the past, and it takes place in the broader context of the battle for the recognition of gay marriage by public authorities and by Davis herself.

If we continue to highlight what or who might carry weight in the conversation without being directly or explicitly present in the scene, we can see, at line 21, Moore asking Davis, "how many times have you been married, Kim?" This question seems out of context, and it may appear so to the uninformed observer. However, the very fact that this question is being asked without being apparently triggered by a previous turn of talk, not to mention the absence of relevant reply from Davis, invites looking for an explanation outside of the direct interactional situation, as otherwise it would appear entirely anomalous. Indeed, if we dig into the history of the public battle between the two parties, we learn from the media that Davis has been divorced twice.

By tapping into Davis's personal past, Moore attempts to undermine her legitimacy with respect to the current issue by dislocating and re-contextualizing the conversation as a broader one regarding marriage. Indeed, by bringing into the interaction biographical elements that Davis would have perhaps preferred to leave at home, Moore appears to position Davis as someone without the necessary authority to judge who should or shouldn't get married, whether they are of the same sex or not. However, this is a strategy that Davis does not seem to be inclined to buy into.

In fact, in line 23, Davis simply replies, "I just want you all to know that we are not issuing marriage licenses today." Davis does not seem to be ready to (re-)contextualize the present conversation. On the contrary, she puts the emphasis on the present time (i.e., the here, the now, and the local), deflecting the previous insinuation about her multiple divorces and, by proxy, lending her back her authority as county clerk. The dislocal move that Moore tried to put in place by bringing back the past appears to be part of a broader strategy to undermine Davis's professional credibility, a credibility that Davis has herself fragmented by allowing her personal beliefs about marriage to come into this issue. In other words, it appears that Moore was looking to highlight the paradox of Davis's identity: on the one hand, she claims to be the county clerk implementing the law—a law now allowing same-sex marriages—but, on the other hand, her refusal to issue a marriage license seems to be driven by her religious beliefs, a supposedly personal aspect in most Western societies. Later in the conversation, in lines 202 and 214–215, Moore explicitly alludes to this by saying that no one has to know the beliefs of others in order to get a license.

As we can see, both parties to the scene produce authority effects by importing past and future events or aspects that, although seemingly absent, nonetheless count in the situation. By doing so, each representative either boosts their own credibility or undermines the other's authority by framing the conversation according to their interests, both in and out of context.

Smiles: A CDA Perspective

Oren Livio

Our third analysis employs Wodak's (2011, 2014) four-level context model described above while bringing into the discussion concepts from Fairclough's (1992) and van Dijk's (2008, 2009) approaches. Let us go back to the very beginning. The interaction begins with Ermold's statement to Davis, "Don't smile at me," to which Davis replies "I did not smile," followed by "I'm not being disrespectful to you." At the level of the immediate textual context (Fairclough, 1992; Wodak, 2014), we can see that there is a back-and-forth character to these utterances. This includes both word repetition or slight variation (e.g., "don't smile"/"I did not smile," lines 3–6; "I'm not being disrespectful"/"You absolutely have disrespected," lines 8–9) and response-based adjacent use of pronouns (e.g., "to you," line 8, followed by "us," lines 9 and 10; "You" in line 10, followed by "I" in line 11, and "you" again in lines 12 and 13).

These immediate textual repetitions and variations establish, first, that we are witnessing a form of ordered dialogue (despite what might be seen as rather chaotic surroundings); and, second, that the tone of this dialogue is confrontational, with each side attempting to deflect the verbal choices made by the other and take control of where the interaction is going. In other words, this is a symbolic battle over power and authority in which seemingly trivial issues such as whether Davis is smiling stand in metonymically for the larger issues being negotiated. This being the beginning of the conversation, it serves as an "orientation . . . and overall structuring device and frame for all upcoming events" (Wodak, 2014, p. 333).

Contextual factors operating at other levels generally reinforce this interpretation while occasionally also complicating it. As our earlier dislocal analysis has demonstrated, third-level extralinguistic cues such as the smile, Ermold's gestures, posture, and tone of voice, as well as the environmental settings that have both sides facing one another, divided by a large desk, also imply conflict. So too does our knowledge of the cultural conventions governing such bureaucratic encounters, particularly the presence of media in the room, which suggests that what we are witnessing is not a routine administrative procedure (that media would have no reason to cover).

In fact, it is the tension between what is considered standard for this type of encounter and what appears to depart from this standard that assists interpretation: we recognize elements of formal hierarchical structure and power relations (e.g., the administrative bureaucrat possesses the power to confer status upon regular citizens)—but also realize through the atypical nature of the proceedings that something about these relations is working differently this time. Thus, while we might initially be tempted to see in Davis's smile a standard symbol of politeness, or perhaps a neoliberal customer-service orientation, a variety of cues both textual and intertextual alert us to realizing that this is merely a façade—albeit one that the participants are determined to enact—leading us to view the entire interaction first and foremost as a performance played out primarily for non-present participants.

Apart from the intertextual references to previous encounters and Davis's previous marriages that have already been analyzed from a dislocal perspective, we might want to also consider here the intertextual reference to "second-class citizens" (line 10) and the accompanying reference to "an interracial couple" (line 17). References to such loaded and historically recognizable terms link the LGBTQ population to other discriminated groups, and in particular to those whose equal legal rights (though not necessarily their actual rights) are for the most part no longer questioned. They thus serve as argumentative strategies (Reisigl & Wodak, 2009) employing commonplace (yet historically specific) "conclusion rules" such as the idea that all citizens should be treated equally and that history will frown upon those who do not do so (see also lines 111–127).

It is here that the broader sociopolitical and historical context is most evident. Here too our interpretation of the text-context relation requires the most background information. For, if only recently (and still so in many places) it was clear who had *more* power in the broader social arena, with gay couples being discriminated against both formally and informally, in at least this specific case Davis appears to be clutching onto power that has become mostly symbolic. Indeed, approximately one year after this interaction, only thirteen U.S. counties were still refusing to issue same-sex marriage licenses, and Davis herself had stopped interfering with their issuing (Johnson, 2016). By June 2018 this figure had declined to nine, of which only one was specifically refusing same-sex marriage licenses, whereas the others had stopped issuing marriage licenses altogether to avoid violating the law (Dunigan, 2018). What was previously an exercise of legally sanctioned governmental power against a discriminated minority could now legitimately—although certainly not only—be seen as an act of protest or even conscientious objection by a local county clerk, and this indeed appears to be how many citizens opposing gay marriage perceived it (Kelly, 2015).

While some outside knowledge is necessary—and relevant—for interpreting the situation, some characteristics of discursive practice (Fairclough, 1992) are also of help; for example, we may observe that all journalists in the room are standing on Ermold's and Moore's side of the desk, implicitly leading us to consider the interaction from their point of view and to be sympathetic to their cause (Kress & Van Leeuwen, 2006). Hart (2015) has demonstrated how such choices in both visual and linguistic discourse lead to different context models that are linked to ideological interpretations. Our understanding of how authority and power are distributed in this interaction is thus informed to some extent by contextual elements (see also Sky Marsen's analysis of media narratives in chapter 6).

Finally, while we do not have any direct evidence for how participants in the interaction interpreted it in their minds—what context models (van Dijk, 2008, 2009) they *actually* developed—we can use textual evidence to at least demonstrate how these models appear to have been different for different participants. To do so, let us go back to the use of pronouns referred to earlier. We have already seen how the use of such pronouns elicits repeated or reverse-mirror pronoun use from respondents (e.g., "I"/"you," "you"/"you," "you"/"us," lines 8–9). But a closer look at these uses reveals that they may also be associated with different context models that participants build and attempt to deploy strategically to direct the interaction in certain ways.

One example of this occurs very early: after Ermold's assertion that Davis is smiling at "me" (line 3) and Davis's response that she did not smile and is not being disrespectful to "you" (line 8)—which might logically be seen as referring to Ermold—he immediately utilizes the inherent ambiguity of the English "you" (which may be either singular or plural) to make the claim that Davis is disrespecting "us" (line 9). This is then picked up by Moore, who claims that she is treating "us" as second-class citizens (line 10) and that she is telling "us" that "*we* don't deserve the same right rights (sic) that *you* do think that *you* have." What is particularly interesting here from a context-centered perspective is that Davis's local, singular "you" is transformed by the couple synecdochally to represent both their joint status as a plural "you" and, more importantly, the gay community in general—as evidenced by the intertextual reference to "we" deserving the same rights as "you" do. "You" and "we" operate here as fuzzy signifiers that may alternately or simultaneously refer to local or universal, individual or group contexts.

In the dislocal analysis above we saw how Ermold and Moore attempt to contextualize the events in terms of Davis's illegitimacy as a moral authority on marriage given her own previous divorces—that is, they attempt to enforce an expanded context model incorporating past and distant events. Davis resists this attempt by emphasizing the here and now—"we are not issuing marriage licenses *today*" (line 23). We can now add to this level the use of pronouns by participants, which attempts to accomplish the same task at the level of grammar. Davis's pronouns are almost exclusively local to the interaction, referring to herself and the people directly in front of her. They thus *contract* context. Conversely, Ermold and Moore use primarily ambiguous, plural pronouns such as "we" and "us" (as well as the fuzzier "you") that serve to collapse the distinction between individual action and collective history and ideology. They thus *expand* context, attempting to place the couple's specific battle within the larger history of intolerance and discrimination.

Conclusion

Any analysis of a text can only signify in the context of something, and is thus generative of context, indexing many more anew (c.f., Jones, 2016; Tracy, 1998). With each analysis, we offered a different lens through which to examine the first twenty-five lines of the interaction, granting authority not just to that which we took to be empirically significant but to the primacy of (a) particular context(s) over others. Table 1.1 crystallizes our theoretical positions and analytical arguments in this chapter; we offer it to summarize that though context is certainly not reducible to an interactional bucket, it nonetheless works as a set of affordances and constraints (Kress & Van Leeuwen, 2001), or what the analyst chooses to fit and leave out, expose and obscure.

Our first analysis uses this very argument to justify itself. By using the metaphors of display and watch, and purporting to expand context from the text itself to the text and its analysts, we attempt to close a hermeneutic circle quite neatly and yet avoid actually addressing our own

Table 1.1 Summary of Analytical Approaches to Context

Perspective	Discourse analysis Mariaelena Bartesaghi	Dislocal perspective Frédérik Matte	Critical Discourse Analysis (CDA) Oren Livio
Analytical focus	Accounts for contexts as multiply embedded matrices of social action	Emphasizes local discursive manifestations as locus for out-of-context evocation	Links local discursive manifestations to broader sociocultural relations of power
How authority is constituted in interaction	Authority is a collaborative and orderly production of an accountable moral order. In offering accounts, participants are engaged in producing a shared text; claiming different positions of accountability with respect to their roles within that text; calling upon available resources to authorize those roles; entextualized, recontextualized, and institutionalized as texts.	Authority is brought to being through participants' evocation of anything that potentially gives weight and makes a difference. Many different beings come to speak and act through interactions, whether these beings be facts, principles, values, rules, emotions, and so on. Instead of remaining local, micro, or limited, any interaction becomes dislocated or "dislocal."	Authority is negotiated through participants' (and analysts') understandings of the relevant characteristics of the interaction, which are shaped by the immediate textual surroundings, intertextual references, extralinguistic environmental elements, and broader sociopolitical and historical conditions.
How it shifts understanding of authority	Authority is an unaccountable reading of a text or a context that is (apparently) locked into place.	Authority is what is *authored*, that is, the multitude of actors of various ontologies that built or created it through discourses and interactions.	Authority is neither completely structural nor completely agentic. It is dynamic and flexible, negotiated throughout the interaction and simultaneously shaped by power and constitutive of power.
Key concepts	Analyst's positioning, reflexivity, authority dynamic, intertextuality, accountability	Constitutive approach, ventriloquism, space-timing, materiality, discursive practice	Ideology, power, text, discursive practice, social practice, intertextuality, context models
Suggested readings	Antaki et al. (2003), Bartesaghi (2015), and Jones (2009)	Fairhurst and Cooren (2004, 2009) and (Cooren, 2010)	Fairclough (1992), Flowerdew (2014), van Dijk (2008), and Wodak (2014)

claims as analysts about the smile and how to be reflexive about them. This remains a problem for the other two analyses and, arguably, for (C) DA more broadly. Whether attempting to construct and perfect a method for transcription and analysis in which the researcher is ideally (and idealized as) nonexistent, as in CA, or more explicitly acknowledging the analyst as part of the context and even considering this an inspired demonstration of the reflexive critical impetus, as in some Frankfurt School informed approaches to CDA (Reisigl & Wodak, 2009; Wodak & Meyer, 2009), both the theorizing and the systematic empirical operationalizing of the analyst's role as- and in-context remain underdeveloped.

It is here, perhaps, that incorporating more ethnographic tools associated with linguistic anthropology and the ethnography of communication may prove useful, a point indeed made by Blommaert (2005) and others. While some discourse analytic methods certainly employ such tools, their use is often pragmatic and limited.

To be sure, this is hardly a straightforward endeavor. In many cases, discourse analysts must grapple with discourses that are "already there," and this is not merely a matter of utility but also of necessity, given our role as watchers of already-present texts, events, and institutions. Some approaches to discourse analysis, such as Tracy's Action-Implicative Discourse Analysis (AIDA, e.g., 2010) that involves extensive fieldwork on everyday practices, or Wodak's DHA (e.g., Reisigl & Wodak, 2009; Wodak, 2014), ordinarily incorporate ethnographic methods, but this sets some limits on what can be studied, how it can be studied, and what time frames are required—limitations that do not always fit researchers' agendas and possibilities.

Or, this might be an argument for what we have not included and may never know how to fully include, even as our fingers are typing this text to materialize the contexts of our analysis: our bodies and the bodies of others. Much like the service counter that both unites and divides the speakers on the scene and all the voices and the figures that are called to speak, present and absent, doing discourse analysis points to the limitations of capturing the sensory. Try as we may to meet the universe halfway (c.f. Barad, 2007) by inviting dislocation, ideologies, and technological displays into our analytical frames, the universe pushes us back. Though we may suspect what is and is not in an interaction, and though we may know it in our bodies, our discourse analyses have not yet provided us with adequate contexts to authorize this knowing.

Notes

1. The volleys spanned a three-year period (e.g., Schegloff, 1997; Billig, 1999), with a follow up by Kitzinger (2000). Not to be missed is Tracy's Forum (1998).
2. We employ DA as an umbrella term to several approaches to language and social interaction (see Stubbe et al., 2003; Tracy, 1998) that consider text and context to be politically and socioculturally entangled.

3. To avoid a strawman argument, we acknowledge that using images together with transcripts is not new. CA, for example, has been studying the gaze to understand how interaction is coordinated since its beginnings.
4. As the clip entreats, "watch Kentucky clerk"—thus setting up different in-the-moment displays, each including different watchers.

References

Antaki, C., Billig, M., Edwards, D., & Potter, J. (2003). Discourse analysis means doing analysis: A critique of six analytic shortcomings. *Discourse Analysis Online, 1*. Retrieved from www.shu.ac.uk/daol/articles/v1/n1/a1/antaki2002002-t.html

Barad, K. (2007). *Meeting the universe halfway: Quantum physics and the entanglement of matter and meaning*. Durham, NC: Duke University Press.

Bartesaghi, M. (2015). Intertextuality. In K. Tracy (Ed.), *International encyclopedia of language and social interaction* (pp. 901–906). New York: Wiley.

Benoit-Barné, C., & Cooren, F. (2009). The accomplishment of authority through presentification: How authority is distributed among and negotiated by organizational members. *Management Communication Quarterly, 23*(1), 5–31.

Billig, M. (1999). Whose terms? Whose ordinariness? Rhetoric and ideology in conversation analysis. *Discourse & Society, 10*(4), 543–558.

Blommaert, J. (2005). *Discourse: A critical introduction*. Cambridge, UK: Cambridge University Press.

Bucholz, M. (2000). The politics of transcription. *Journal of Pragmatics, 32*(10), 1439–1465.

Bucholz, M. (2007). Variation in transcription. *Discourse Studies, 9*(6), 784–808.

Buttny, R. (1993). *Social accountability in communication*. London: Sage.

Context. (2019). *Merriam-webster dictionary*. Retrieved from www.merriam-webster.com/dictionary/context

Cooren, F. (2010). *Action and agency in dialogue: Passion, incarnation and ventriloquism*. Amsterdam: John Benjamins.

Dunigan, J. S. (2018). Three years after Supreme Court ruling, at least 8 Alabama counties won't issue marriage licenses. *AL.com*. Retrieved from www.al.com/news/birmingham/index.ssf/2018/06/three_years_after_supreme_cour.html

Fairclough, N. (1992). *Discourse and social change*. Cambridge, UK: Polity Press.

Fairhurst, G. T., & Cooren, F. (2004). Organizational language in use: Interaction analysis, conversation analysis, and speech act schematics. In D. Grant, C. Hardy, C. Oswick, & L. Putnam (Eds.), *The Sage handbook of organizational discourse* (pp. 131–152). London: Sage.

Fairhurst, G. T., & Cooren, F. (2009). Leadership as the hybrid production of presence(s). *Leadership, 5*(4), 469–490.

Flowerdew, J. (2014). Introduction: Discourse in context. In J. Flowerdew (Ed.), *Discourse in context* (pp. 1–25). London: Bloomsbury.

Fox, B. A. (2012). Conversation analysis and self-repair. In C. Mortensen & J. Wagner (Eds.), *The encyclopedia of applied linguistics*. Cambridge, MA: Wiley-Blackwell. https://doi.org/10.1002/9781405198431.wbeal0214

Garfinkel, J. (1967). *Studies in ethnomethodology*. New York: Prentice-Hall.

Goffman, E. (1983). The interaction order. *American Sociological Review, 48*(1), 1–17.

Grimshaw, A. D. (Ed.). (1990). *Conflict talk: Sociolinguistic investigations of arguments in conversation*. Cambridge, UK: Cambridge University Press.

Hart, C. (2015). Viewpoint in linguistic discourse. *Critical Discourse Studies,* *12*(3), 238–260.

Iedema, R. (2011). Discourse studies in the 21st century: A response to Mats Alvesson and Dan Kärreman's "Decolonializing discourse". *Human Relations, 64*(9), 1163–1176.

Johnson, C. (2016, June 22). One year after marriage ruling, pockets of defiance remain. *Washington Blade.* Retrieved from www.washingtonblade.com/2016/06/22/ one-year-after-supreme-court-ruling-pockets-of-marriage-inequality-remain/

Jones, R. H. (2009). Technology and sites of display. In C. Jewitt (Ed.), *The Routledge handbook of multimodal analysis* (pp. 114–126). London: Routledge.

Jones, R. H. (2016). *Spoken discourse.* London: Bloomsbury.

Kelly, A. (2015, September 26). Kim Davis' supporters, in their own words: "Courageous", "heroic". *NPR.* Retrieved from www.npr.org/sections/itsallpolitics/ 2015/09/26/443485200/courageous-heroic-meet-kim-daviss-supporters

Kitzinger, C. (2000). Doing feminist conversation analysis. *Feminism & Psychology, 10*(2), 163–193.

Korobov, N. (2001). Reconciling theory with method: From conversation analysis and critical discourse analysis to positioning analysis. *Forum: Qualitative Social Research, 2*(3). Retrieved from www.utsc.utoronto.ca/~kmacd/IDSC10/ Readings/text%20analysis/CDA.pdf

Kress, G., & Van Leeuwen, T. (2001). *Multimodal discourse: The modes and media of contemporary communication.* London: Edward Arnold.

Kress, G., & Van Leeuwen, T. (2006). *Reading images: The grammar of visual design* (2nd edition). London: Routledge.

Ochs, E. (1979). Transcription as theory. In E. Ochs & B. Schieffelin (Eds.), *Developmental pragmatics* (pp. 43–72). New York: Academic Press.

Petitjean, C., & González-Martínez, E. (2015). Laughing and smiling to manage trouble in French-language classroom interaction. *Classroom Discourse, 6*(2), 89–106.

Reisigl, M., & Wodak, R. (2009). The discourse-historical approach (DHA). In R. Wodak & M. Meyer (Eds.), *Methods of critical discourse analysis* (2nd edition, pp. 87–121). London: Sage.

Robles, J. S., & Castor, T. (2017, May). *Taking the moral high ground: Avoiding accounts as a practice for being uncompromisingly principled.* Paper presented at the International Communication Association, San Diego, CA.

Schegloff, E. A. (1997). Whose text? Whose context? *Discourse and Society, 8*(2), 165–187.

Schegloff, E. A. (2000). On granularity. *Annual Review of Sociology, 26,* 715–720.

Scollon, R. (1998). *Mediated discourse as social interaction: The study of news discourse.* London: Longman.

Stubbe, M., Lane, C., Hilder, J., Vine, E., Vine, B., Marra, M., Holmes, J., & Weatherall, A. (2003). Multiple discourse analyses of a workplace interaction. *Discourse Studies, 5*(3), 351–388.

Taylor, J. R., & Van Every, E. J. (2000). *The emergent organization: Communication as site and surface.* Mahwah, NJ: Lawrence Erlbaum.

Tracy, K. (1998). Analyzing context: Framing the discussion. *Research on Language and Social Interaction, 31*(1), 1–28.

van Dijk, T. A. (1977). *Text and context.* London: Longman.

van Dijk, T. A. (2008). *Discourse and power.* New York: Palgrave Macmillan.

van Dijk, T. A. (2009). Critical discourse studies: A sociocognitive approach. In R. Wodak & M. Meyer (Eds.), *Methods of critical discourse analysis* (2nd edition, pp. 62–86). London: Sage.

Vásquez, C., & Cooren, F. (2013). Spacing practices: The communicative configuration of organizing through space-times. *Communication Theory, 23*(1), 25–47.

Watch Kentucky clerk defy Supreme Court on gay marriage. (2015, September 1). *USA Today*. Retrieved from www.usatoday.com/videos/news/nation/2015/09/03/71527640/

Wetherell, M. (1998). Positioning and interpretive repertoires: Conversation analysis and poststructuralism in dialogue. *Discourse & Society, 9*(3), 387–412.

Wodak, R. (2011). *The discourse of politics in action: Politics as usual* (2nd edition). Basingstoke: Palgrave.

Wodak, R. (2014). Political discourse analysis: Distinguishing frontstage and backstage contexts: A discourse-historical approach. In J. Flowerdew (Ed.), *Discourse in context* (pp. 321–345). London: Bloomsbury.

Wodak, R., & Meyer, M. (2009). Critical discourse analysis: History, agenda, theory and methodology. In R. Wodak & M. Meyer (Eds.), *Methods of critical discourse analysis* (2nd edition, pp. 1–33). London: Sage.

Wooffitt, R. (2005). *Conversation analysis and discourse analysis: A comparative and critical introduction*. London: Sage.

2   The Varieties of (More or Less) Formal Authority

Alena L. Vasilyeva, Jessica S. Robles, Jean A. Saludadez, Christian Schwägerl, and Theresa Castor

The chapter examines how power and formal authority are interactionally achieved. In this respect, the study follows research on interactional power and authority in institutional contexts, for example, radio talk (Hutchby, 1996), therapy sessions (Bartesaghi, 2009), and dispute mediation (e.g., Tracy & Spradlin, 1994). This work extends the arguments of the aforementioned studies to analyzing the interactional achievement of *formal* authority and challenges traditional assumptions about the nature of formal authority. Our overarching focus is on discourse as language-use in social interactions. However, as our group discussed and analyzed the data, we found that we had different, albeit complementary, insights that we gained based on more specific analytic lenses that we were applying.

This divergence in analysis is illustrative of how discourse analysis can be applied in multiple ways. Alena Vasilyeva, Jessica Robles, and Christian Schwägerl focused more on the details and "mechanics" of the language-use in applying discourse analytic and conversation analytic approaches. Jean Saludadez and Theresa Castor tended to notice the different ways conflict parties were in practice "speaking on behalf of" others as they applied a ventriloquial approach. Therefore, an additional objective of this chapter is to illustrate three specific ways to examine language in interactions: through discourse analysis, conversation analysis, and a ventriloquial approach. In the following sections, we will briefly touch upon the differences between formal and informal interactions; discuss the research on constitutive approaches to authority and power; illustrate the use of discourse analysis, conversation analysis, and a ventriloquial approach to studying formal and informal varieties of power and authority; and finally compare these alternative perspectives in terms of methodological and theoretical implications and contributions.

Formal Versus Informal Interaction

A common theme in our approaches is attention to language-use in naturally occurring interactions. This calls for attending to patterns within and across conversations and making inferences about what such patterns mean for broader issues such as identity, relationships, and/or culture. To illustrate what is involved in paying attention to such patterns, we describe findings related to conversational differences in formal versus informal interactions. This contrast was also selected given the relevance of formal interactions to our case study.

First, we will address formality as an empirical matter in interaction. Within the framework of conversation analysis, Atkinson (1982) points out that there is a distinction in the production of orderliness in an ordinary conversation (e.g., a chat with a friend) and settings that are considered to be "formal" (i.e., non-conversational) such as courtroom interaction, parliamentary proceedings, and church services, to name a few. Some features of formal talk that researchers can attend to include but are not limited to topics appropriate to discuss, kinds of actions participants may perform and their design, the length of pauses between the turns, possibilities for repair, the construction of particular identities, asymmetries in power and knowledge, and turn-taking constraints (e.g., Atkinson, 1982; Drew & Heritage, 1992; Sacks, Schegloff, & Jefferson, 1977).

For example, in an ordinary conversation, participants take turns interchangeably (i.e., the order of turns is not fixed); there are short pauses between turns and brief if any turn overlaps. In formal talk, turns may be pre-allocated (Sacks et al., 1977); that is, an order of speaking may be known in advance. Besides, there might be a party (e.g., mediator, moderator, judge) who makes decisions as to who should speak next, which is known as turn-mediation (Atkinson, 1982).

Another feature of turn-taking systems in formal contexts is turn-type pre-allocation (Atkinson, 1982), that is, the restrictions on what type of actions participants can perform in a particular turn. One more aspect that distinguishes formal talk from an ordinary conversation is the content of interaction. While in ordinary conversation participants can discuss various topics and shift freely from one topic to another, in more formal talk, there may be constraints on what can be discussed. There are also particular distributions of knowledge that are oriented to in institutional encounters, marked by references to status and position, that might be seen as a way of enacting forms of authority (Mondada, 2011). In the next section we consider institutional authority and power in more detail.

Authority and Power

While power and formal authority are interconnected notions, it is important to keep in mind the distinction between them, given that "having" formal authority does not necessarily mean that one is able to exercise power. The assumption that this distinction matters is shared across the approaches applied in this chapter: power is generally understood as "a personal ability to influence the behavior of other people (usually against their will)" (Chiang, 2015, p. 1), while formal authority can be defined as "an act of influence perceived to be 'right' because it is in concordance with existing and accepted organizational structures" (Benoit-Barné & Cooren, 2009, p. 6) such as institutional rules, roles, and practices. Taylor and Van Every (2014) note that while power and authority are commonly linked in the research literature, little work has been done to clarify their relationship, with few empirical studies that actually examine "authority in practice" (p. xviii).

In attending to discourse as language-use in interactions, our group also shared a constitutive perspective regarding formal authority. In contrast to Max Weber's (1958) traditional view of formal authority as derived from a position a person has, the constitutive approach to authority and power emphasizes the collaborative achievement of authority as created and maintained through interaction (e.g., Benoit-Barné & Cooren, 2009; Chiang, 2015; Heritage & Raymond, 2005; Koschmann & Burk, 2016; Koschmann, Kopczynsky, Opdyke, & Javernick-Will, 2017; Pomerantz & Denvir, 2007). For example, Koschmann et al. (2017) underline the idea of authority as a process by illustrating how a single organization, namely Young Pioneer Disaster Response (YPDR), communicatively constructs their authority in times of disaster in the Philippines. First, the organization expresses their authority in terms of local people's appreciation. Second, they show "their ability to act authoritatively in terms of government officials that supported their work" (p. 11). Finally, when they become well known among other organizations, they express their authority in terms of their expertise and ability to collaborate with other agencies.

Discourse analytic researchers are also interested in how various communicative practices are employed to construct authority and power in interaction (e.g., Bartesaghi, 2009; Benoit-Barné & Cooren, 2009; Goodwin, 1990; Griswold, 2007; Hutchby, 1996; Maoz & Ellis, 2001). In various institutional contexts such as meetings, interactants may have access to the same interactional resources to establish power (Maoz & Ellis, 2001). Some key discursive practices for accomplishing authority and power include metalinguistics, institutional positioning, authorizing emotions and actions, and how talk is sequentially organized (for example, coming in first or second position offers relative benefits and detriments to advancing or defending positions in arguments; see Hutchby, 1996). While most research focuses on how discursive strategies are used to achieve power and authority, it is equally important to address actions of subordinate parties in interaction, as they are engaged in co-construction of authority and power (see, for example, Griswold, 2007).

Discourse analytic approaches tend to take a constitutive approach to authority and power and underline their dynamic character; for example, research on parliamentary debates (e.g. Ilie, 2003; van Dijk, 2004) shows how linguistic, contextual, and rhetorical features of the interaction accomplish a particular adversarial genre including formal properties (such as members' roles and positions), as well as discursive patterns and metadiscursive conventions. Interactants do not necessarily treat authoritative attributes as pre-existing and fixed but as matters of negotiation in interaction. In the next sections, we demonstrate how the methods of discourse analysis, conversation analysis, and the ventriloquial approach are employed to analyze the same data to understand the construction of formal and informal varieties of power and authority. Jessica, Christian, and Alena introduce discourse analytic and conversation analytic approaches, while Theresa and Jean take a ventriloquial perspective.

Discourse Analysis of Formal and Informal Authorities

Jessica Robles, Christian Schwägerl, and Alena L. Vasilyeva

In this section we focus on how Davis and others enact formal and informal varieties of authority by managing local institutional roles and duties (such as provision of marriage licenses), attempting to claim interactional power over the course of the conversation, and referring to dislocated institutional authorities (such as God or the police). We focus on the formal and informal dimension of institutional power: how participants manage, claim, resist, and transform sources of authority that may be formal (such as an institutional role) or informal (such as controlling the direction of talk). Our analysis examines participants' discursive strategies to show that who has authority and power is constantly negotiated in this interaction. We start with a general discourse analytic approach (Tracy, 2001) that analyzes participants' social actions and how features of language-in-use contribute to interactional meaning.

Though "discourse analysis" (DA) is a label that can describe many different ways of analyzing talk or text, in studies of communication, what discourse analytic approaches typically share is an interest in how talk is accomplished in context, for what particular local goals, and how certain acts achieve such aims, present people's identities, and frame situations in different ways (Cameron, 2001; Tracy, 2001). Discourse analysis involves recording, transcribing, and analyzing actual instances of communication for features such as speech acts, style, linguistic and nonverbal details, storytelling, and so forth; different ways of doing discourse analysis emphasize different ways of examining discourse (Cameron, 2001).

The local institutional context and the tasks and roles it entails provide accessible legitimizing resources for both sets of participants in this interaction: those on the service side of the counter, including Davis, and those who, if not actively agreeing with her, tacitly support her denial of service; and those on the customer side of the counter, which include couples seeking marriage licenses as well as members of the press. In this interaction, interactional power is interwoven with the institutional speech acts and practices the participants enact.

For example, Davis, by virtue of her role, is responsible for issuing licenses or not and enacts this by making an announcement in line 23 ("I just want you all to know that we are not issuing marriage licenses today"). In addition to having the (in this case, contested) ability to provide or deny licenses, she also shifts the scope of recipients of her talk from Moore to all present in the room ("you all"). Second, by shifting from personal "I" to an institutional "we," she indicates that she acts in her formal institutional role. Third, she makes reference to "marriage licenses," thus redirecting the conversation from personal matters (i.e., her marriage, which was at stake just prior) to institutional matters.

Davis also attempts to control the flow of the conversation by initiating certain activities (her announcement on line 23 provides her an opportunity to close the interaction) and responding (or not responding) in particular ways. This illustrates how power does not stay constant in the course of interaction but shifts from one participant to another depending on the moves they perform. In this example, participants seem to be competing for interactional power. While attempting to take certain actions, participants also seek to resist the actions of others.

Davis resists the institutional requirements to ignore her religious stance (occasioned by the appearance of Moore and Ermold to obtain a license but also by their articulated demands) by not complying with Moore and Ermold's requests. Though she uses the language of the institution, she is in fact not doing her job by framing Moore and Ermold not as legitimate seekers of a marriage license but as disruptors of "business as usual." She uses various strategies to perform as though not participating in the "spectacle" of what is going on, even as she also contributes to it: for example, by using institutional language, politeness markers, and organizational framing (e.g., of the interaction as a service encounter in which services may be refused). On the surface, Ermold and Moore conduct themselves as though they are merely seeking a license. It becomes clear, however, that they are also doing something else, namely, they are making this interaction about an unfairness with which they have been dealing.

Another way in which participants manage interactional authority is by formulating their actions in certain ways. For example, at times they do what looks like institutionally appropriate "demanding" (such as Davis's refusal of service and Ermold's demands to be issued a license), and this is a way of claiming the authority to do such acts. At other times, however, actions are packaged with politeness markers that might suggest one is doing "trying to be reasonable" or casting the other as "unreasonable." For example, in lines 238–241, Ermold makes an unsuccessful attempt to ask Davis a question. Rather than asking the question directly, Ermold makes a request to perform this action (lines 238 and 240). The use of the phrase "let me ask," and the addition of "please" when his first attempt fails, on the surface seems to ratify Davis's authority to allow Ermold or deny his right to ask questions. Simultaneously it is also a way in which Ermold does being aggrieved and "attempting to keep one's patience." Davis does not grant him permission and initiates termination of the conversation ("We're done" in lines 239 and 241). Ermold's language enacts him as a polite person, and, in contrast, Davis's actions to reject his request depict her as bullying.

The moment where Davis initiates termination of the interaction and withdraws from it (see lines 89–94) is the most extreme example of attempting to control the interaction. In line 89, Davis demands those present to clear the area in front of the counter. In line 90, Ermold refuses to leave the office without getting a license. Davis, in line 92, warns Ermold that they will have to wait a long time to get it. In line 93, a person from the crowd demands Davis to do her job. However, Davis ignores the demands and instead says goodbye and leaves towards a room at the back (line 94), thus withdrawing from the interaction completely. Instead of producing a relevant response, Davis opens a new activity (namely, a farewell sequence) and withdraws from interaction: in this way she enacts her interactional power again. In an asymmetric relationship, usually a person who has a higher position is more likely to terminate interaction without providing any explanation. For example, it is the chairperson who initiates the closing of the meeting (Pomerantz & Denvir, 2007).

In managing the local institutional encounter and the way it unfolds in the interaction, participants also manage and invoke relevant institutional authorities, some of which are local, many of which are distant. For example, Davis invokes her position of power by mentioning her business ("I've asked you all to leave, you are interrupting my business" in lines 55–56) and her territory ("just push back away from the counter" in line 86). She makes an attempt to enforce institutional rules, which appear to be that if a customer disrupts work in the institutional setting, an institutional agent has the right to restore the institutional order, for example, by asking this person to leave.

The legitimacy of Davis to enact this authority is challenged in different ways. In lines 57 and 59, Moore indirectly questions Davis's authority to enforce rules on them by making a reference to the police as the legitimate (legal) power that can force them to leave (legal authority versus institutional authority of the particular organization; e.g., "You can call the police if you want us to leave" in line 57). Another client in line 58 directly undermines Davis's authority by pointing out that it is not her business ("It's not your business"), thus denying her the right to enact institutional authority. Finally, Moore enacts his institutional role of a client and a taxpayer in lines 63 and 65 (e.g., "I'm paying you your salary" in line 63). By pointing out that he pays Davis's salary, he introduces the rights of a client by referring to the fact that he is a tax-payer (line 63), thus counterbalancing Davis's moves and placing himself in a superior position.

Finally, there is a clash between legal and moral authorities, which is performed by other forms of agency and authorship: the court versus God. While the court may be invoked as a formal authority—one to which citizens are compelled to submit based on explicit rules—God's authority is open to interpretation based on whether one believes in God or not, the extent to which that belief assumes intervention into human lives, and so forth. God may have been a common and traditional form of authority through most of history, but, as demonstrated in the data here, that form of authority may be rejected or even deemed inapposite in contemporary modern life in favor of the rational-legal approach taken by courts and the justice system (see Weber, 1958).

While Davis appeals to the authority of God to justify her refusing to register marriage, Moore and others appeal to the decision of the court as a legitimate authority. It is noteworthy that Davis's claim is challenged from different angles. First of all, Moore expresses doubt that Davis acts on behalf of God (e.g., "Did God tell you to do this? Did God tell you how to treat us (.) like this?" in line 52). Second, Ermold denies the existence of this authority ("I don't believe in your god" in line 53). Finally, the relevance of this authority in this matter is called into question (e.g., "God (.) does not belong in the county clerk's office" in line 130). In the next section we consider how a more sequentially focused, conversation analytic approach to institutional talk (Heritage, 2005) might see these phenomena in slightly different ways.

Conversation Analysis of Formal and Informal Authorities

In this section we take up many of the practices described in the previous section, but reanalyze them from a more sequential perspective, drawing on ethnomethodology and conversation analysis to show how Davis resists the authority of the courts and Moore and Ermold's demands; while Moore and Ermold resist Davis's attempts to assert her institutional role and her invocations of God's authority. As a qualitative method, conversation analysis (CA) examines the audible verbal and paraverbal as well as observable nonverbal practices of speakers at a fine-grained level of detail that involves highly specific methods of transcribing recorded conversation (see Hepburn & Bolden, 2013). CA assumes that conversations are sequentially ordered (Sacks, Schegloff, & Jefferson, 1974). Technically, the method dissects these activities into single turns which again can be structured into sequences of actions (e.g., greeting and greeting, invitation and acceptance or rejection of the invitation) in the form of larger conversation structures and other features of spoken communication (e.g., pauses, embodiment, and vocalics) and inspects the reciprocal nature of talk by investigating the ways speakers orient to each other in their communicative practices.

CA elaborates on this reciprocity by looking at the interplay of sequential order of parts of the conversation and the specifics of timing and speaker change as well as lexical, syntactical, phonological, and prosodic features to bring out how speakers' activities collaboratively create mutual understanding and meaning. This can be achieved, for example, by examining the emergence of activities that assume a particular interactional relevance in subsequent turns: the "next turn proof procedure" (Schegloff, 2007). CA bases analysis on observable communicative practices and defines meaning as action. Attempts to exercise power and authority count as interactionally accomplished when they are ratified or rejected in the participants' subsequent turns (e.g., Pomerantz & Denvir, 2007). For example, in a classroom setting, it is usually a teacher, a figure of formal authority, who controls turn-taking and sequence organization (Gardner, 2013). But an interactant's deontic authority (i.e., the right to make decisions) is challenged when the recipient does not comply with the initiated action, thereby showing deontic incongruence (Stevanovic & Peräkylä, 2012). This incongruence is evident when the recipient treats the speaker's announcement of some decision as news rather than displays commitment to the action, thus pressuring the speaker to provide an account for the decision.

Also, CA assumes that understanding and meaning result from participants' orientation to each other. This requires cooperation in the sense that participants share communicative resources and share inferences when interpreting prior utterances and designing their activities against the local context. Meaning, understanding and "accomplishments" are based, in this view, on participants' inferencing work rather than on denotational, "fixed" meanings of terms and concepts: "To interact, as conversational analysts have shown, is to engage in an ongoing process of negotiation, both to infer what others intend to convey and to monitor how one's own contributions are received," Gumperz notes (1999, p. 454). This process of co-construction also relies on participants' demonstrated background knowledge commonly used in a specific extrasituational context, such as in an institutional setting. We suggest that in its turn-by-turn technical approach, CA has the capacity to elicit the local situated meaning of abstract concepts, such as "second-class citizen," "being disrespectful," and "authority."

We begin by questioning the distinction between forms of institutional or noninstitutional authority. In our analysis so far, we have implied that there are formal authorities at work (specific institutional roles and bodies such as the local county clerk's office, the courts, and the police) but also informal authorities such as participants' interactional practices (though these are often vested in formal invocations). Instead we now ask, under what circumstances are actions "formal" or oriented to by participants as such?

Furthermore, we can reanalyze the opening sequences of the interaction without recourse to assumptions about what the participants are trying to do and without assuming power and authority are omnirelevant. The turn-by-turn analysis of communicative practices may shed light on the participants' subjective understandings and presuppositions the speakers associate with related concepts such as "authority" and "power." The situation opens when Davis enters the service area of the office, with Ermold, Moore, and the uncounted number of people standing behind the service desk. Ermold starts with the loud and clearly articulated "don't smile at me" (line 3), followed by Davis's "I did not smile" and a pause of two seconds.

The following exchange of turns exhibits the participants' varying presuppositions of *disrespect*. Whereas Davis does not elaborate on "I'm not being disrespectful to you" (line 8), Ermold's and Moore's partly overlapping "you absolutely have disrespected us" (line 9) and "you absolutely are, treating us as second-class citizens" (line 10) can be read as an "account" (Heritage, 1988), an explanation of and reference to the current speaker's preceding utterances. Here, Moore first objects to Davis's "I'm not being disrespectful." In a reading of "you absolutely are, treating us second-class citizens" (line 10) and the subsequent "telling us that we don't deserve the same right rights that you do think that you have" (lines 12–13), Moore contrasts an understanding of "being disrespectful" with the sense of "being treated equally."

Also, the context-dependent inferencing processes that underlie concepts related to the notion of authority—such as "disrespectful"—are exhibited in the interactive consequences, i.e., subsequent utterances or turns that display the ways speakers understand preceding utterances (c.f. Schegloff, 1992; see also Gumperz, 1999). They are also exhibited in turns that are produced in the second or third position (Schegloff, 1992). In this view, Moore's "is what you are doing, telling us that we don't deserve the same right rights that you do think that you have" in lines 12–13 can be seen as a response to Davis's "I'm not being disrespectful to you," which challenges her authority.

We can also examine participants' apparent "attempts to control the floor" or "attempts to enact interactional power" by refocusing on how the participants redirect and interrupt the sequential organization of the interaction. This was done, for example, by not providing a relevant response and even withdrawing from interaction. In the episode that unfolds in lines 17–23, Moore shapes the sequential organization of the interaction by asking Davis questions ("Would you do this to interracial couple?" in line 17 and "How many times have you been married, Kim?" in line 21), thereby initiating sequences; by doing the "first pair part" of interaction (i.e., an utterance initiating exchange, such as inquiry and invitation), Moore sets the sequential context of the interaction (Cameron, 2001). While, in line 19, Davis responds by providing a second pair part (i.e., an utterance responsive to the action of a prior turn, such as answer and rejection) to the question of whether she would behave in the same manner toward an interracial couple or not, in line 23, she does not a provide a relevant type-conforming response and thus makes a sequential shift in the interaction by instead initiating a new sequence. An appropriate answer in this situation would be saying how many times she was married. However, to do so would concede her position, and indeed, the question may not be a "question" at all; it may be a "rhetorical" question that does not demand a literal response but instead makes a point about the untenability of Davis's actions (see Reynolds, 2011). At the same time, it may be interpreted as her attempt to enact her formal role of a clerk, as the first question is related to her responsibilities, while the second one is not. In this sense, this passage is of particular interest. Davis refuses to answer a question that we can conceive of as very personal ("How many times have you been married," line 21). Rather than responding to it, she refers to her formal institutional role as a clerk in the subsequent "we are not issuing marriage licenses today," with the pronoun "we" moving her formal institutional role in the foreground.

Rather than seeing these profferings of dispreferred non-type-conforming responses and attempts to initiate new sequences through the lens of participants' intentions to occupy positions of power, an interactional perspective focuses on how the disaligned activities derail the progressivity of the interaction. What we might analytically call "conflict," "disagreement," or a "battle for power" are set aside to focus on the machinery of their production. Part of how such visible antagonisms are produced is through disaligning actions—there may or may not be explicit, on-record disagreement, but participants can resist responding in expected ways or initiate new sequences instead of responding to the current one. In doing so, they contest the terms under which responding to the current activity is reasonable, proposing instead a different sort of social action: Davis resists the authority of the courts and Moore and Ermold's attempts to gain compliance from her, while Moore and Ermold resist Davis's treatment of the interaction as an institutional problem (rather than an ideological one). The next section presents a different approach to these matters in interaction, considering not just who speaks but also how "nonhumans" acquire agency.

Ventriloquial Analysis of Formal Authority

Theresa Castor and Jean Saludadez

Whereas the conversation analytic approach focused on the features of talk that contributed to the conflict and its impasse, the ventriloquial approach helps in understanding how different background agents informed and shaped the present conversation, enabling us to see how formal authority and its constitution itself is a matter of dispute. In this section, we explicate and illustrate how to apply a ventriloquial approach.

The ventriloquial approach sees communication as "not only a matter of people speaking or writing to each other, but that other things are continuously inviting and expressing themselves in day-to-day interactions" (Cooren, 2011, p. 11), thereby including "other things" (i.e., nonhumans) as agents. Being an agent means being able to act or speak "on behalf of principal" (Taylor & Van Every, 2000, as cited in Cooren, 2006, p. 82). Figures and agents "are the very conditions of our authorities and power because they lend weight to our positions" (Cooren, 2010, p. 27). This approach assumes that "various sources of authority—understood as forms of agency—can be invoked or mobilized in a given interaction or dialogue" (Cooren, 2010, p. 75), suggesting that authority is a shared accomplishment. This approach also transforms our understanding of formal authority from one that locates authority within a position to one in which formal authority is a communicative accomplishment where a legitimizing institution is made "present" or "materialized" in interaction (Benoit-Barné & Cooren, 2009). In this respect, the formal authority associated with an individual is "authorized" and "authored" by a prior institutional agency.

In applying a ventriloquial perspective, Benoit-Barné and Cooren (2009) state that authority is accomplished through *presentification*, "that is, by making sources of authority present in interaction" (p. 5). Benoit-Barné and Cooren note that sources of authority are not necessarily limited to individuals but can include collectives, documents, and ideas, among others, showing how authority is distributed across different agents.

Another important aspect of a communicative view of authority and power is that these are not restricted to agents who present themselves as *a priori* in authority but can be acquired in interaction (Benoit-Barné & Cooren, 2009). For example, Benoit-Barné and Cooren illustrate how power and authority are achieved in interaction between a medical coordinator of the organization Médecins Sans Frontières (MSF) and a technician from a hospital that is supported by MSF. The coordinator positions herself as a person who has organizational authority to speak on specific processes and to criticize the work of the unit. The technician meanwhile shifts the coordinator's authority to himself by constructing an imbalance in terms of actions. The technician first indicates that they honored the coordinator's directive in regard to the hospital procedures, which seemingly puts the coordinator in the position of debt. Following along with the ventriloquial perspective that Benoit-Barné and Cooren apply, this allows the technician to speak in the name of his coworkers and to introduce their problem. According to Benoit-Barné and Cooren, it is "a certain form of justice or fairness in the name of which he dares to speak" (p. 24) and gives him authority to speak.

A ventriloquial analysis entails a three-step process. The first step, recording interactions as they happen or collecting recorded interactions, is common across all of our approaches. However, the following two steps are specific to a ventriloquial approach. The second step is to identify markers through which a variety of figures appear to recurrently and iteratively express themselves in the interactions. The third step is to interpret or make inferences about what the figures are made to say (or do).

There are different forms of authority, as the chapters in this collection have illustrated. Our analysis emphasizes formal authority as based on the person's position in the organizational hierarchy, but challenges it by showing that this position must be made interactionally present in each situation in order to gain authoritative effect. We therefore focus our ventriloquial analysis on Kim Davis's formal authority as it is highlighted or emphasized in comments that reference her organizational authority. Kim Davis "has" formal authority in the interaction based on her formal organizational position (i.e., job). However, formal authority does not necessarily mean having power over others, given that an individual in a position of formal authority is obligated to fulfill the expectations of her role (an issue that is repeatedly made explicit in the conflict episode).

In implementing a ventriloquial approach, the sources of authority invoked/incarnated/mobilized by the county clerk and how they are made situationally relevant can be "surfaced" through Table 2.1.

Davis fortified her authority through configuring the following:

- The collectives (the use of "we" and the reference to "people")
- The institutional procedure (the use of "appeal" and the reference to the "governor")
- The constitutional right to religious freedom (the religious "choice" and the reference to "God")

By enrolling a collective, mobilizing an institutional procedure, and invoking a constitutional right, Davis made present the unseen sources of formal authority in order to perform a decision-making role (approval or disapproval of an application in this case). Made relevant as sources of authority, these sources are positioned as co-authoring the act of not issuing marriage license to gay couples.

While in one respect, Davis's formal authority can be viewed in terms of her position, there were ways that the protestors challenged her construction of formal authority, peeling away to reveal the supporting institutional and personal layers that animated Davis's action. The protestors did this by ventriloquizing other formal "sources" of authority that they spoke on behalf of or by attempting to demand that Davis ventriloquize her role in specific ways.

In line 39, Davis falls into a "customer-service script" as she states, "we are not issuing marriage licenses today," a statement that she reiterates two lines later (line 41) after Ermold tries to counter her refusal by referencing the institutional authority of the Supreme Court. As part of a "customer-service script," an organizational representative has the

Table 2.1 Davis Ventriloquizing Formal Authority

Markers/figures	Analysis on what the figure is trying to do
"WE are not issuing licenses today" (lines 23, 39, 41)	"We" stands for the collective (office) and is made to say that issuing the license is an institutional act and refusal to issue the license is not an individual prerogative.
"Pending the APPEAL." (line 30)	The "appeal" is an indirect reference to the court. The figure of the court is made to say that the office's refusal to issue the license is allowable as a matter of procedure.
"GOD's authority" (line 49)	In a conflation of different forms of authority (traditional and formal), this statement implies that "God" is authorizing her NOT to issue licenses: Davis is thereby acting as an agent on behalf of God.
"PEOPLE can't get in here . . . Just push back AWAY FROM THE COUNTER" (lines 61 and 86)	By "materializing" the counter, Davis makes the office setting relevant for the interaction: the office has other business at hand and, while the gay couple are taxpayers, there are other taxpayers equally needing attention. She is therefore acting on behalf of other clients.
"=You believe passionately in wh[at you are doing as I do" (line 156) "That's your CHOICE" (lines 201, 218)	This figure of "choice" is made to say that one's religious choice does not deter one from running for office nor quitting office and performing one's job. Davis therefore piggybacks on Moore's own previous invocation of the figure of choice to state that she is authorized to have her personal beliefs in the name of that same figure.
"We're done here . . . there is a remedy . . . If the GOVERNOR would do . . . " (lines 239, 255, 257)	This figure of the governor's office is made to say that while Davis's office does not issue licenses, gay couples can obtain a license from other county offices or through an action of a higher governing body. Davis thereby seems to attempt to cast both the couple's and her situation as being attributable to a common figure, namely the governor.

authority to refuse service to customers (see Robles & Castor, 2019). Davis's use of this script indirectly draws on her formal authority in that, as an organizational representative and therefore someone who can (i.e., is authorized to) ventriloquize the script, she may refuse to provide service to a customer. Davis also ventriloquizes the organization: the script signals that she is just an employee following prescribed guidelines of how employees are authorized to deal with customers. In this respect, Davis positions herself as a ventriloquial dummy who is animating an institutional script without agency of her own.

Ermold then challenges Davis by asking directly "based on what?" (line 42) and then again, "why are you not issuing marriage licenses today?" (line 44). At which point, she steps outside of her formal role as organizational representative by citing "God's authority" (lines 49–50).

In lines 55–56, she reverts back to her organizational authority and customer-service script, and at this point, Ermold and others start to dissect Davis's formal chain of authority. Someone in the audience counters, "it's not your business" (line 58), thereby challenging Davis's authority to ventriloquize the "business." Davis's authority as an organizational representative is further challenged when David and others dissect her chain of authority (Castor & Cooren, 2006):

```
63   MOORE   [I'm paying you your salary ((repeatedly pointing his index at her))
64           (0.5)
65   MOORE   I PAY YOUR SALARY ((repeatedly pointing his index at her and raising his
66           voice))
67           ((Kim Davis makes a look expressing a form of surprise))
68   OTHER   We pay your salary
```

In stating that they "pay" her salary, Ermold and others highlight how Davis's formal authority is based on her position as a public employee whose salary is paid for through taxpayer money. Therefore, it is her duty, within her formal role, to carry out certain actions, including the federally approved legal duty now of allowing same-sex couples to wed. This is reiterated again in line 82 after White states, "I'm asking you to do your job," and lines 93, 96, 102, 145, and 176 as others (unidentified) demand, "Do your job!" There are two implications of the demands that Davis "do her job." First, Ermold and others dissect the basis for how organizations are constituted not just in the immediate presence but through a chain of associations that provide the basis for formal authority. Second, in highlighting this basis of authority, David and others can be said to ventriloquize the voice of authority of the organization in pointing out what they see as an inconsistency between Davis's actions and the requirements of her position within that context. Thus, the capacity to voice formal authority is not the sole possession of the individual who occupies the position of formal authority.

The ventriloquial approach shows how formal authority is an accomplishment that is distributed across different agents (Benoit-Barné & Cooren, 2009). Some of these can be construed as relevant for Davis's formal authority as a clerk. However, Davis's authority—by her own admission—was driven by other sources such as her religious beliefs. In this respect, Davis enacted a hybridized, polyphonic form of authority (Castor & Cooren, 2006) consisting of multiple voices (see Bakhtin &

Emerson, 1993). The ventriloquial approach focuses on the figures that are made relevant by interlocutors in constituting authority. In applying a ventriloquial approach to this conflict interaction, the analysis illustrated how formal authority is not the property of an individual but rather can be communicatively constituted by any interlocutor.

Discussion

This chapter illustrated three analyses of varieties of (more or less) formal authority in interaction: discourse analysis, conversation analysis, and ventriloquial analysis. The analyses look at authority and power as interactional accomplishments and matters of negotiation for participants in talk-in-interaction. While it may appear that, formally, Davis is a figure of authority in the examined interaction due to her institutional position, the analyses show that this is not necessarily the case if we look at how the interaction unfolds moment to moment.

In organizations, the fixed institutional order may formally legitimate professions, roles, and official duties. Formal status, however, is not a fixed variable in interaction that speakers solely orient to in their verbal activities in institutional settings. DA allows us to examine how people can display and resist institutional roles and activities, enacting various sorts of identities in the process and framing their talk for different (even cross) purposes. Thereafter we applied CA to reconstruct the participants' demonstrated understandings of "authority" as sequences of action. For an interactant to exercise authority, it is important that the addressees align with this person's actions (Stevanovic & Peräkylä, 2012). However, Davis's authority and power are constantly challenged as the addressees take incongruent actions. According to Stevanovic and Peräkylä (2012), to show deontic incongruence, the interactants produce "responses that are atypical to the first pair-parts" (p. 309). A conversation analytic method, in this respect, has an advantage, as it focuses on the sequential organization of talk and allows us to see whether the recipients perform type-conforming responses. For example, the conditionally relevant response to Davis's request to leave the office would be to comply with the request (a preferred response) or refuse to comply (a dispreferred one). While the dispreferred response itself indicates the recipient's disalignment and challenges the speaker's authority, Moore also performs an action (i.e., a directive, "You can call the police," framed as giving permission) that is not a type-conforming response.

The ventriloquial approach focuses on the figures that are made relevant by interlocutors in constituting authority. Formal authority can be ventriloquized directly or metacommunicatively (i.e., as topic of discussion). As Taylor and Van Every (2014) note, when there is a disagreement on authority, organization breaks down. In the case of the conflict interaction studied here, interlocutors oriented to different sources of authority (Davis's "job,"

Table 2.2 Summary of Analytical Approaches to Formal Authority

Perspective	Discourse analysis Jessica Robles, Christian Schwägerl, and Alena L. Vasilyeva	Conversation analysis Heritage, J. Vasilyeva and Alena L. Vasilyeva	Ventriloquial approach Theresa Castor and Jean Saludadez
Analytical focus	discursive practices; function of talk	the structural organization of talk; sequence of actions	how human and nonhuman beings speak on behalf of others
How authority is constituted in interaction	language-in-use positions or claims authority among participants	through subsequent turns, rights are accepted or challenged	invoking figures to legitimize one's actions
How it shifts understanding of authority	authority as a dynamic process negotiated in interaction	authority as an interactional and collaborative achievement	authority is "authored" and positioned within a stream of action
Key concepts	social action, activity types, language-in-use, talk in context, discursive strategies, discursive markers, negotiation of meaning	adjacency pair (first-pair part, second-pair part), turn design, social action, sequence organization, preference organization	ventriloquism, communicative, constitution, presentification, narrative, textual agency
Suggested readings	Cameron, D. (2001). *Working with spoken discourse.* Thousand Oaks, CA: Sage. Tracy, K. (2001). Discourse analysis in communication. In D. Schiffrin, D. Tannen, & H. E. Hamilton (Eds.), *The handbook of discourse analysis* (pp. 725–749). Malden, MA: Blackwell.	Heritage, J. (2005). Conversation analysis and institutional talk. In K. Fitch, & R. Sanders (Eds.), *Handbook of language and social interaction* (pp. 103–147). Hove, UK: Psychology Press. Heritage, J., & Raymond, G. (2005). The terms of agreement: Indexing epistemic authority and subordination in talk-in-interaction. *Social Psychology Quarterly,* 68, 15–38. Stevanovic, M., & Peräkylä, A. (2012). Deontic authority in interaction: The right to announce, propose, and decide. *Research on Language and Social Interaction,* 45, 297–321.	Cooren, F. (2010). *Action and agency in dialogue: Passion, incarnation and ventriloquism* (Vol. 6). Amsterdam: John Benjamins. Cooren, F. (2012). Communication theory at the center: Ventriloquism and the communicative constitution of reality. *Journal of Communication,* 62(1), 1–20. Cooren, F., & Sandler, S. (2014). Polyphony, ventriloquism, and constitution: In dialogue with Bakhtin. *Communication Theory,* 24(3), 225–244.

"God," federal law, etc.). With specific reference to *formal* authority in terms of institutional positioning, interlocutors disagreed on what figures should take precedence in how Davis's formal authority should be constituted, with Davis narrowly focusing on her "job" and Ermold and others addressing her responsibilities within the context of the recent court ruling.

In applying conversation analytic, discourse analytic, and ventriloquial approaches, we note that they are compatible in illustrating how varieties of formal authority are negotiated through language-use in social interactions. Where they differ is in the aspects of conversation that they attend to, with DA analyzing identities and discursive strategies, CA focusing on conversational sequence and how participants orient to institutional rules, and the ventriloquial approach examining how authority is accomplished in a topical and content-oriented way, focusing on direct and indirect references to sources of authority. DA and ventriloquial approaches noted how institutional language was used to navigate complying and not complying with local expectations, as well as the different ways legitimacy was enacted. On the other hand, DA and CA have more in common with each other in terms of examining interaction—CA in particular focuses on turn-by-turn actions—while ventriloquial analysis can examine a single utterance.

For all of the methods applied herein, "authority" is grounded in participants' actions: what they say and do. Even the extent to which authority is "formal" is negotiated and performed, reproduced and resisted, in the participants' local organization of their activities. These perspectives on more or less formal varieties of authority may emphasize different mechanisms for how authorities are made relevant (e.g., in the display of identities and framing of talk versus the sequential organization of actions versus the distribution of voiced content across agents), but share a common social constructionist critique of authority as something that is obviously located in particular persons or roles.

References

Atkinson, J. M. (1982). Understanding formality: The categorization and production of "formal" interaction. *British Journal of Sociology, 33*, 86–117.

Bakhtin, M. M., & Emerson, C. (1993). *Problems of Dostoevsky's poetics*. Minneapolis, MN: University of Minnesota.

Bartesaghi, M. (2009). How the therapist does authority: Six strategies for substituting client accounts in the session. *Communication & Medicine, 6*, 15–25. doi: 10.1558.cam.v5i2.15.

Benoit-Barné, C., & Cooren, F. (2009). The accomplishment of authority through presentification: How authority is distributed among and negotiated by organizational members. *Management Communication Quarterly, 23*(1), 5–31. https://doi.org/10.1177%2F0893318909335414

Cameron, D. (2001). *Working with spoken discourse*. Thousand Oaks, CA: Sage.

Castor, T., & Cooren, F. (2006). Organizations as hybrid forms of life: The implications of the selection of agency in problem formulation. *Management Communication Quarterly, 19*(4), 570–600. https://doi.org/10.1177%2F089 3318905284764

Chiang, S. Y. (2015). Power and discourse. In K. Tracy, C. Ilie, & T. Sandel (Eds.), *The international encyclopedia of language and social interaction* (pp. 1–17). Boston, MA: John Wiley & Sons. doi: 10.1002/9781118611463.wbielsi149.

Cooren, F. (2006). The organizational world as a plenum of agencies. In F. Cooren, J. R. Taylor, & E. J. Van Every (Eds.), *Communication as organizing: Empirical and theoretical explorations in the dynamic of text and conversation* (pp. 81–100). Mahwah, NJ: Lawrence Erlbaum.

Cooren, F. (2010). *Action and agency in dialogue: Passion, incarnation and ventriloquism.* Amsterdam: John Benjamins Publishing Company.

Cooren, F. (2011, May). *Figures in tension in organizational communication.* Paper presented at the 61st Annual Conference of the International Communication Association, Boston, MA.

Drew, P., & Heritage, J. (1992). Analyzing talk at work: An introduction. In P. Drew & J. Heritage (Eds.), *Talk at work* (pp. 3–65). Cambridge, UK: Cambridge University Press.

Gardner, R. (2013). Conversation analysis in a classroom. In J. Sidnell & T. Stivers (Eds.), *The handbook of conversation analysis* (pp. 593–611). Oxford, UK: Blackwell Publishing Ltd.

Goodwin, M. H. (1990). *He-said-she-said: Talk as social organization among Black children.* Bloomington, IN: Indiana University Press.

Griswold, O. (2007). Achieving authority: Discursive practices in Russian girls' pretend play. *Research on Language and Social Interaction, 40,* 291–319. https://doi.org/10.1080/08351810701471286

Gumperz, J. J. (1999). On interactional sociolinguistic method. In S. Sarangi & C. Roberts (Eds.), *Talk, work and institutional order: Discourse in medical, mediation and management settings* (pp. 453–471). Berlin and New York, NY: Mouton de Gruyter.

Hepburn, A., & Bolden, G. B. (2013). The conversation analytic approach to transcription. In J. Sidnell & T. Stivers (Eds.), *The handbook of conversation analysis* (pp. 57–76). Oxford, UK: Blackwell Publishing.

Heritage, J. (1988). Explanations as accounts: A conversation analytic perspective. In C. Antaki (Ed.), *Understanding everyday explanation: A casebook of methods* (pp. 127–144). Beverly Hills, CA: Sage.

Heritage, J. (2005). Conversation analysis and institutional talk. In K. Fitch & R. Sanders (Eds.), *Handbook of language and social interaction* (pp. 103–147). Hove, UK: Psychology Press.

Heritage, J., & Raymond, G. (2005). The terms of agreement: Indexing epistemic authority and subordination in talk-in-interaction. *Social Psychology Quarterly, 68,* 15–38. https://doi.org/10.1177%2F019027250506800103

Hutchby, I. (1996). *Confrontation talk: Arguments, asymmetries, and power on talk radio.* Mahwah, NJ: Lawrence Erlbaum Associates, Publishers.

Ilie, C. (2003). Discourse and metadiscourse in parliamentary debates. *Journal of Language and Politics, 2*(1), 71–92. https://doi.org/10.1075/jlp.2.1.05ili

Koschmann, M. A., & Burk, N. R. (2016). Accomplishing authority in collaborative work. *Western Journal of Communication, 80,* 393–413. https://doi.org/1 0.1080/10570314.2016.1159728

Koschmann, M. A., Kopczynsky, J., Opdyke, A., & Javernick-Will, A. (2017). Constructing authority in disaster relief coordination. *The Electronic Journal of Communication/La Review Electronic de Communication, 27*, 1–24.

Maoz, I., & Ellis, D. G. (2001). Going to ground: Argument in Israeli-Jewish and Palestinian encounter groups. *Research on Language and Social Interaction, 34*, 399–419. https://doi.org/10.1207/S15327973RLSI3404_01

Mondada, L. (2011). The management of knowledge discrepancies and of epistemic changes in institutional interactions. In T. Stivers, L. Mondada, & J. Steensig (Eds.), *The morality of knowledge in conversation* (pp. 27–57). Cambridge, UK: Cambridge University Press.

Pomerantz, A., & Denvir, P. (2007). Enacting the institutional role of chairperson in upper management meetings: The interactional realization of provisional authority. In F. Cooren (Ed.), *Interacting and organizing: Analyses of a management meeting* (pp. 31–51). Mahwah, NJ: Lawrence Erlbaum Associates, Publishers.

Reynolds, E. (2011). Enticing a challengeable in arguments. *Pragmatics: Quarterly Publication of the International Pragmatics Association (IPrA), 21*(3), 411–430. https://doi.org/10.1075/prag.21.3.06rey

Robles, J. S., & Castor, T. (2019). Taking the moral high ground: Practices for being uncompromisingly principled. *Journal of Pragmatics, 141*, 116–129. https://doi.org/10.1016/j.pragma.2018.12.015

Sacks, H., Schegloff, E. A., & Jefferson, G. (1974). A simplest systematics for the organization of turn-taking for conversation. *Language, 50*, 696–735.

Sacks, H., Schegloff, E. A., & Jefferson, G. (1977). The preference of self-correction in the organization of repair in interaction. *Language, 53*, 361–382.

Schegloff, E. A. (1992). Repair after next turn: The last structurally provided defense of intersubjectivity in conversation. *American Journal of Sociology, 97*(5), 1295–1345.

Schegloff, E. A. (2007). *Sequence organization in interaction: Volume 1: A primer in conversation analysis* (Vol. 1). New York, NY: Cambridge University Press.

Stevanovic, M., & Peräkylä, A. (2012). Deontic authority in interaction: The right to announce, propose, and decide. *Research on Language and Social Interaction, 45*, 297–321. https://doi.org/10.1080/08351813.2012.699260

Taylor, J. R., & Van Every, E. J. (2000). *The emergent organization: Communication as site and surface*. Mahwah, NJ: Lawrence Erlbaum Associates, Publishers.

Taylor, J. R., & Van Every, E. J. (2014). *When organization fails: Why authority matters*. New York, NY: Routledge.

Tracy, K. (2001). Discourse analysis in communication. In D. Schiffrin, D. Tannen, & H. E. Hamilton (Eds.), *The handbook of discourse analysis* (pp. 725–749). Malden, MA: Blackwell.

Tracy, K., & Spradlin, A. (1994). "Talking like a mediator": Conversational moves of experienced divorce mediators. In J. P. Folger & T. S. Jones (Eds.), *New directions in mediation: Communication research and perspectives* (pp. 110–132). Thousand Oaks, CA: Sage.

Van Dijk, T. A. (2004). Text and context of parliamentary debates. In P. Bayley (Ed.), *Crosscultural perspective on parliamentary discourse* (pp. 339–372). Amsterdam: John Benjamins Publishing Company.

Weber, M. (1958). The three types of legitimate rule. *Berkeley Publications in Society and Institutions, 4*(1), 1–11.

3 How Institutional Authority and Routine Exertions of Power Can Be Mobilized, Negotiated, and Challenged

Helle Kryger Aggerholm, Birte Asmuß, Geneviève Boivin, Richard Buttny, and Klaus Krippendorff

Institutions consist of widely accepted, largely routinely enacted, and basically impersonal social practices. In organizational contexts, they include functional definitions of offices, articulated procedures, routines, protocols, rules, policies, etc. that collectively tend to survive the lives of those enacting them. Institutional authority derives from the power assumed by office holders to control particular social practices.

The contributors to this chapter develop a variety of concepts by which the emergence, enactment, and demise of authority and power routines could be understood. It consists of four individual analyses of the video which pursue different perspectives that nevertheless share a number of features regarding the nature and practice of authority:

1. We see authority as residing in social processes. It occurs neither in the psychology of individuals nor in individual action. Instead, authority is an intersubjective phenomenon. As such it is *interactively co-constructed*, negotiated, or maintained. Authority cannot exist without cooperation or compliance. It is a discursively evolving social construct.

2. Authority becomes observably evident in how participants coordinate their turns-at-talk and respond to each other's actions. This includes all processes by which participants direct each other's attention, define their participation, and influence or control what is ongoing among them. It suggests that authority and power are *processual* in nature, emerging through the multiple, ongoing, interactional negotiations between the different participants.

3. We conceive of authority not only as constituted in verbal interactions, but also as *multimodally* accomplished, including through smile, gaze, hand gesture, and body position. These take place in physical spaces where they are enacted, in our case the counter that separates county employees and their clients (see Figure 3.1); unequal access of material resources (computers, records of past

interactions, enforced office hours, appointment schedules, etc.), all of which provide the contexts in which authority is interactively constructed.

4. We acknowledge authority to be *publicly* enacted. There always are witnesses or bystanders, whether in view of the interlocutors known to have the ability to enter ongoing exchanges, or omnipresent in the form of microphones, video cameras, official records, or signed documents that could affect the meanings of the ongoing interactions at a later point in time. While the recorded participants could not anticipate what we as absent witnesses would do, they certainly interacted in the awareness of a potentially large public attributing meanings to what they did.

5. Our fifth commonality concerns the data we are utilizing to understand the interactive construction of authority. We are committed to ground our contributions in the contextualized interactions we can observe and ideally record for careful examinations. Given the points mentioned above, transcriptions of verbal interactions are important but are greatly enhanced by *video-observations* (LeBaron, 2008), as these to a higher degree than textual or audio data enable the analyst to study organizational phenomena as a *member's phenomenon* in that the array of resources used in the data is closely though not fully covered by video data.

6. While nobody can escape the social implications of communication, including the abstractions that come with the use of natural language, we prefer to *proceed from the bottom up*, tying our explanations as closely as possible to the actual interaction as opposed to letting abstract social theories frame our interpretations.

7. Finally, we are aware that our interpretations put us in the position of witnesses outside the recorded interactions. None of us were present at the encounter, and our accounts could not participate in what we are analyzing. However, unlike conventional scientific accounts of social phenomena, the above commonalities entail awareness that our interpretations can retrospectively affect how readers judge the participants named in this encounter and prospectively shape their own interactions in similar situations. This entails assuming responsibilities for how our scholarship could shape the future of what we are analyzing. While this reflexivity is implicit in all contributions to this chapter, they differ in what is important to them.

This chapter begins with a ventriloquial analysis of how actors negotiate the authority of figures through interaction. Ventriloquism, defined as "the phenomenon by which an actor makes another actor speak through the production of a given utterance" (Cooren, 2010, p. 1), challenges the traditional notion of an individual authorship, the latter being instead conceptualized as a shared accomplishment by accounting for anything that makes a difference in the interaction or that plays a part in a given situation.

The second analysis examines the social accountability of authority and how it is mobilized, negotiated, and challenged. Communicators continually attend to what they and their interlocutors are doing and the propriety of those actions. The social accountability of action becomes most visible as talk or positions are called into question or problematized. A blame, complaint, or question from another makes relevant an account to deny, excuse, explain, or justify oneself. The encounter at the county clerk's office comprises a number of argumentative statements invoking social accountability which constitutes much of the conflict. This analysis attempts to uncover the discursive practices in doing authority and social accountability. Social accountability is central to establishing or questioning authorities in social organizations, drawing upon social and moral norms and thereby reinforcing or modifying organizational and institutional structures.

The third analysis assumes a critical and constructive perspective. It considers accountability as the ability and willingness to account for one's assertions or actions to those requesting explanations, justifications, or apologies, usually in view of untoward situations. Accounts are speech acts that, when provided, enable participants in social encounters and analysts like us to identify perceptions, motivations for actions, and options considered or rejected. In the process of negotiating acceptable accounts, human agency is socially constructed or denied. As a discursive practice, accountability enables confirming or challenging claimed authorities, complying with or undoing burdensome exertions of power, and reinforcing or modifying social institutions and organizational forms.

In the fourth analysis, the present encounter sheds light on how organizational routines on a micro-level contribute to the accomplishment of larger organizational routines, thus how the micro-level of interaction and the macro-level of organizational life are interrelated in and through interactions. This contribution proposes a multimodal conversation analytic approach focusing on the performative aspects of organizational routines. This approach reveals how procedures and routines in interaction can serve as a resource for the participants to accomplish specific organizational goals and thereby to achieve a position of power and authority on an institutional level.

Figure 3.1, already mentioned, offers a snapshot of the encounter of our analytical attention. It illustrates the physical space in which authority is enacted, challenged, and analyzed by us. It depicts the physical barrier in the form of a counter between the space occupied by the county clerk's office staff and the one occupied by citizens expecting to be served. On the left side we can recognize some of the resources of the county office—computers, printers, files, and chairs for employees to sit and do their work—absent on the right side where citizens have to stand. While

Figure 3.1 Participants

arguing, the participants assume variously attentive positions, including making gestures and facial expressions.

In the fifth analysis, this critical perspective is extended to the practices of social scientists who, if their published theories are socially relevant, can be expected to participate in subsequent constructions and enactments of the very social realities they describe. Scientific authority should not be immune to criticism by those theorized, affected by or making use of its claims. Critical social scientists ought to be wary of proposing abstract causal theories that imply uncontestable objectivity aimed at preventing being challenged by their stakeholders.

While all five approaches to understanding the emergence, practices of and challenges to authority are grounded in observable interpersonal interaction, their analytical focus varies widely.

Negotiating Authority Through Ventriloquism

Geneviève Boivin

What could be more mundane than someone getting a license at a government office? If someone wants to get married, he/she has to have a license, just like if he/she wants to hunt or drive. It is a technical document that recognizes a right to do something, and it is usually acquired through institutionalized processes that are rarely contested. But what happens when the actors involved in these practices challenge the institution at play? The interaction between Kim Davis, David Ermold, and David Moore provides us with an interesting case to explore the way actors negotiate through interaction established practices that usually "offer powerful guides, even constraints for organizing" (Lammers & Barbour, 2006, p. 371). By doing so, they are also negotiating who/what rightfully has a say in the process of getting a marriage license and "make speak" specific figures (Cooren, 2010, 2012) that supposedly have authority on the matter: that is, the federal court and God, both mobilized in the name of interests, beliefs, and values.

To explore this particular theme, I rely on a ventriloquial approach grounded in Cooren's (2010) work. I show how figures, defined as the discursive and material features that populate actors' conversations, discourses, and actions, are mobilized to orient who and what has authority in this interaction. Cooren explains that when someone or something speaks on behalf of something or someone else, that person or artifact is, in fact, sharing the authorship with *who* or *what* he/she is ventriloquizing. In short, "ascribing authority to something or someone usually consists of identifying *who* and *what* is authoring something at a specific moment" (Cooren, 2010, p. 73, emphasis in original). In the following paragraphs, I will show how the actors discursively mobilize specific figures to not only give authority to their statements and actions but also to contest the authority and legitimacy of the actors mobilizing them.

At the beginning of the interaction, Kim Davis challenges the established practice of acquiring a marriage license when she makes the rather assertive claim that "we are not issuing marriage licenses to[day=" (line 23). Interestingly, she does so by relying on the authority of the federal court because of the appeal of the Sixth Circuit that is, according to her, still pending (line 30). She is here speaking on behalf of the institutionalized rules of the federal court of appeal, which allows her to make such an assertive statement. By ventriloquizing the federal court, she is not only giving authority to her refusal to issue the marriage license but also giving weight to her refusal to comply with what others expect to be her role as a county clerk.

However, what is particularly interesting in the unfolding of this interaction is that David Ermold and David Moore, in turn, also ventriloquize the federal court to contest the authority Davis has given herself through the institutionalized figure. By stating the fact that the appeal stay has been denied at line 31, Ermold is also talking in the name of the same institution to challenge Davis's authority which now no longer holds because the figure she had been evoking from the start is now "telling her," according to Ermold, that she *has* to issue marriage licenses. The authoritative figure she herself brought into the interaction now seems to be acting upon her by "*forcing her*" to comply with her role and to issue the marriage license, a position that Ermold explicitly exposes.

Yet, instead of adjusting herself with the rules of the institution she has been ventriloquizing from the beginning of the interaction, she then mobilizes another force to legitimize and justify her (in)action (line 42 to 53). Davis turns to the figure of God and the belief system it represents in her eyes to give weight to her position. Moore and Ermold then once again undermine the authority of the figure she is mobilizing by questioning the beliefs that that she associates with it. By evoking God in the first place, Davis seems to be relying on the authority of a figure that does not approve of gay marriage. David Moore immediately retorts, "Did God tell you to do this? Did God tell you to treat us (.) like this?" By doing so, he is challenging the fact that Davis's actions are authorized by God, and he may be implying that the figure of God is in fact benevolent and non-discriminatory. If God does not discriminate, then the beliefs Kim Davis associates with the figure do not hold. Moreover, the couple further undermines the authority God holds in this interaction by later stating that God does not have a place in this office, thus going back to the practices associated with the clerk office. In other words, if Davis cannot rely on God's authority, she then must comply with her role as county clerk.

Institutionalized practices are often taken for granted. Yet, as we see in this interaction, they can also be challenged and contested. In this analysis, I highlight how the actors do so by not only evoking (explicitly or implicitly) specific figures but also negotiating the authority these figures grant them in this interaction. This allows them to influence the outcomes of the supposedly routinized practice at play.

Mobilizing, Negotiating, and Challenging Authority: On Being Socially Accountable

Richard Buttny

Being accountable for one's actions is a constitutive feature of society; it is part of the social contract and normative order (Scott & Lyman, 1968). Social actions are potentially accountable, especially when they deviate from norms or are unexpected. Most of the time our actions are understood in routine, taken-for-granted ways, and no accounts are called for or given. Social accountability practices, such as blaming another or explaining oneself, implicitly involve institutional, interpersonal, legal, ethical, or religious orders which can be heard as the basis for the accounting. Of course, one may not offer an account when it is called for by another, but this absence may be noticed by others and reflect on the actor's stance or character. Accounts for action function to explain oneself, to reframe the problematic event, and to restore the interaction order among participants.

In this interaction we see attempts to appeal to normative orders in various ways: through explicit or implicit appeals to various institutional authorities, such as county policy, the right to marry, judicial decisions, or even God's authority. Throughout this transcript there are numerous challenges made of the clerk that implicate social accountability and compose this conflict. This interaction can be seen as invoking these different levels of authority based on different normative orders.

Taking our charge as identifying "moments where sources of authority are implicitly or explicitly mobilized, negotiated, and challenged," I adopt a social accountability of communication perspective to focus on the discursive practices in which these aspects of authority are interactionally made socially accountable (Buttny, 1993). Social accounting occurs throughout this encounter, but I limit myself to lines 23–56 since this segment contains arguably the most memorable moments of the exchange.

County Clerk Davis invokes institutional authority by her controversial announcement, "I just want you all to know that we are not issuing marriage licenses today" (line 23). This announcement is a way of getting down to the business of the office given the gay couples and the media assembled at the counter and the events of the previous days. Davis's announcement is an abrupt shift from her immediate prior exchange with Moore and Ermold (lines 1–21). Davis's announcement occurs after the challenging query from an overhearing participant at line 21 about Davis's past marriages. The story of Davis's past marriages presumably was gleaned from news coverage of this conflict. This query of Davis's marriages, along with addressing her by her first name, can be heard as a retort or a moral challenge to her refusal to issue marriage licenses for gay couples—in a sense holding her socially accountable. Davis avoids responding to this challenge at 21 but instead switches footings to address Moore and Ermold and the assemblage at the counter with the announcement of not issuing marriage licenses. Her refusing to respond to the challenging query at line 21 displays her authority as clerk.

Davis's announcement raises the question of how a rule or policy gets applied to a particular situation. That is, what justification does Davis draw on her announcement of "not issuing marriage licenses"? As she attempts to justify her announcement, she is immediately questioned and overlapped (lines 23–27). Davis supports her stance by the account, "Pending the appeal of the Sixth Circuit" (line 30). Davis and her interlocutors' exchange (lines 28–37) show that they recognize being accountable to the courts. They report differing interpretations of how the courts actually ruled, but they align in drawing on the courts as a source of legitimate authority. As this argumentative exchange unfolds, Davis appears unable to rebut Moore's explanation of the courts' induction order (line 37). Davis exerts authority by simply repeating her announcement of not issuing marriage licenses (lines 38–39). Her inability to answer Moore's induction order claim is noticeably absent and is again immediately challenged by Moore overlapping her and citing the Supreme Court's decision. Again Davis is unable to rebut Moore's claim and simply resorts to repeating her announcement one more time (lines 40–41). While Davis can exert authority without answering her challengers, it is hearably a sign of the weakness of her position that she cannot rebut or justify her stance especially given the overlistening assemblage at the counter. In order words, the absence of justificatory account hearably undermines the legitimacy of Davis's stance in the eyes of the applicants.

Davis's announcement is further challenged by Moore and Ermold continuing to hold her accountable for having no legitimate justification for her refusal to issue marriage licenses. This excerpt is a critical moment for understanding their diverging accounts.

```
44   Moore    [Why are you [not issuing marriage licenses today?
45            (0.5)
46   Davis    Because (.) I'm not
47   Ermold   Under [whose authority? (0.5) are you not issuing [licenses?
48   Moore          [Why
49   Davis                                                      [Under God's authority
```

In making her initial announcement, Davis draws on the power of the office in using the first-person plural pronoun *we*: "*we* are not issuing marriage licenses today" (line 23, emphasis added), and likewise in repeating this announcement at lines 39 and 41. In being called to account yet again, she uses first person singular (line 46). Ermold, in response, rephrases Moore's challenge at 47, more explicitly and legalistically calling for an account. Davis then justifies her policy by using Ermold's term "authority" and invoking "God's authority" (line 49), thereby bringing the argument to a whole other level.

So we now have these different sources of justification: the county clerk office, the courts, and now God. The participants all tacitly concur on the courts as authority, thereby providing legitimacy through consensus, but they obviously differ over the relevance of God in this context. As we see, "God's authority" is challenged (lines 51–54). Davis avoids addressing the "God's authority" account and instead shifts footings by attempting to move the gay couples from the counter. The larger point here being that while authority can be invoked at various levels, it also can be challenged through discursive accountability practices. Authority is only as legitimized as justifications that support it in our social and normative orders. Here consensus was not reached though the parties do agree on the need for some authority to authorize a marriage policy.

Relying on Accountability to Establish Agency and Challenge Authority and Powers

Klaus Krippendorff

In the video and transcript of these interactions, the first claim of authority is uttered in the form of a *declaration*: Davis's assertion that "We are not issuing marriage licenses today" (line 23). A declaration is one of several well-researched speech acts capable of constituting realities by naming them, like declaring war, bankruptcy, or being guilty of a crime. However, merely issuing a declaration may not accomplish anything. One preparatory condition for declarations to bring about what they name is for addressees to *accept the speaker's implicitly claimed authority* to issue them. Another is that addressees possess the necessary resources to act accordingly. Declarations remain empty unless their addressees blindly or willingly comply and defer their choices to the speaker, whether as holder of an office, recognized expert, or idolized leader.

We can distinguish three sources of authority: institutional, interpersonal, and rhetorical. An institution consists of widely expected, routinely enacted, and basically impersonal rules and practices. As a county clerk, Davis is responsible for conducting herself as everyone in her position would be expected to, but can do so only as long as the institution she is ventriloquizing is accepted by everyone concerned. A second source is interpersonal, for example, acknowledged expertise or admiration, none of which is evident here. The third source is rhetorical, presenting compelling reasons.

Davis adds rhetorical strength to her declaration by issuing it in the name of the "*we*" (lines 23, 39 and 41) of the members of her staff, and indeed they silently comply. However, her declaration is directed to the applicants for a marriage license who do not comply and try to hold her accountable for issuing this declaration. *Accountability* is the ability and willingness to offer accounts about one's assertions or actions to those demanding them. Offering accounts is quite common. They may be offered by proponents of actions in anticipation of objections (Mills, 1940) or in response to questions by those affected (Shotter, 1984).

Accounts may take the form of explanations (correcting a misunderstanding), excuses (denying agency regarding the questioners' concerns), justifications (elaborating the virtues of a proposal or action), or apologies (admitting responsibility for an untoward situation, promising not to repeat what caused it, and perhaps offering restitution). Accounts are speech acts. Requesting them always disrupts routine consensual practices. They invoke a shift from institutionalized practices to talking among real human beings *about* what they did or didn't do, what could and didn't happen, or the harm they caused. This shift from communication to *meta-communication* is also a shift from relying on institutional practices to interpersonal ones. Conversation analysts frame it as a move to *repair* untoward situations. Activists consider it a way to challenge institutional practices normally not dared.

Accepting given accounts always settles whether a speaker had *agency*, conceived of as having had choices among alternative causes of actions. Justifications and apologies imply agency, excuses deny it. Refusing to accept given accounts leaves the question of agency open to further accounting practices and may lead to the disintegration of consensual expectations. Acknowledged superiors may demand that their subordinates be accountable to them for the job they are assigned to do. The option of giving accounts or refusing accountability to those requesting an answer to the prototypical why-question reveals the *relational asymmetry of authority*—who speaks as an authority and who submits to it.

In response to Davis's declaration, Ermold and Moore, the applicants for a marriage license, demand she explain "*why*" she declared not to issue marriage licenses. Initially, Davis does not respond to their request, merely repeating her declaration, implying that she, as the county clerk, is not accountable to Ermold and Moore, who are mere clients of her office. Based on previous denials of a marriage license and interpreting Davis's smile as disrespectful to their plight (line 9), Ermold and Moore appeal to equal rights of gay and interracial couples and question Davis's qualifications to judge others' entitlement to be married, having been married several times (lines 10–21). Davis continues to claim her institutional authority by not responding to these personal challenges. However, she is interrupted by another why-question (line 24), to which she responds by deferring her agency to a pending appeal in the Sixth Circuit Court. Ermold corrects her interpretation of that court's ruling by claiming that the appeal to stay has been denied by the Supreme Court (lines 33–34 and 40). It is debatable whether Davis acknowledges this fact by nodding. However, Ermold's questioning of her interpretation of the court's ruling she claims to comply with does not prevent her from repeating her declaration (lines 38, 39, and 41).

With Davis's deference to a court's authority dismissed as false, Moore renews the why-question (line 48), to which Ermold adds specificity by asking: "Under whose authority are you not issuing licenses?" (line 47). Davis eventually answers "Under God's authority" (line 49). Denying agency by invoking causes not under one's control is the dictionary definition of an *excuse*. A court of law accepts excuses such as accidents; lacking physical, cognitive, or informational resources; or being under the command of superior agencies.

Deferring One's Agency to Abstractions, Institutions, Canonical Texts, Majorities, Laws, or Ultimate Values Is a Questionable Way to Substantiate Excuses

When speakers defer their agency to a superior authority, to a boss or a trusted expert, subjects may be able to trace the line of deferrals to their source from which speakers claim to be ventriloquized and hold the initiator of that line accountable. However, deferring one's agency to abstractions, shared values, moral principles, ideologies, or doctrines can hardly substantiate an excuse. *Abstractions are discursive constructions* that speakers adopt at will or mindlessly practice. Abstractions cannot speak, write, and be held accountable for their claimed governance. Deferring one's agency to God may well be rhetorical strategy to render one's agency beyond scrutiny. Accepting such deferrals presupposes sharing the belief in the controlling power of these abstractions and locating them outside the participants' ability to hold them accountable.

However, Moore seems astutely cognizant that abstractions have no agency by asking Davis sarcastically: "Did God tell you to do this? Did God tell you how to treat us?—like this?" (line 52). Ermold adds his denial of God to be a mutually accepted authority by asserting, "I don't believe in your God" (line 53), and, later, responding to McKinney by claiming that "We're praying for God and God's word and find solace" (line 129) and "God does not belong in the county clerk's office" (130), echoed by other unidentified voices, "God doesn't run the government!" (lines 132, 133) and "This is not the house of God!" (line 135).

In conclusion, by holding Davis accountable for her declaration and not accepting her effort to defer her agency to higher authorities, Ermold and Moore practice a profoundly clear conception of authority as a challengeable social construction. Evidently, claims to have privileged access to commanding voices, possessing superior abilities, or merely executing social norms can be questioned as such. The supposed power of authorities can be exerted only over consenting subjects. Ermold, Moore, and their supporters did not comply and instead tried to turn the asymmetry of authority around by saying, "We pay your salary" (line 86), followed by multiple voices shouting, "Do your job."

In the end, Ermold and Moore and another couple did not succeed in getting their marriage license during the recorded episode. However, two days later a judge found Davis in contempt of court and ordered her jailed. In 2018, Ermold ran for the Democratic bid for the position of chief clerk of Rowan County, the office occupied by Davis, but Elwood Candill, Jr., became the Democratic candidate and won the office.

Power and Organizational Routines: A Multimodal Conversation Analytical Approach

Helle Kryger Aggerholm and Birte Asmuß

To the extent that organizational practices are institutionalized, they are mindlessly executed routines, repetitive practices, and patterns of interactions, carried out by multiple actors (Dionysiou & Tsoukas, 2013, p. 181; Feldman & Pentland, 2003, p. 95). Traditionally, organizational routines are identified as sociomaterial accomplishments containing both ostensive (ideal or schematic form) and performative (actual production) aspects. Several studies have pointed out that organizational routines inevitably involve "relations of power" (e.g. Feldman, 2000). However, relatively limited attention has been given to power dynamics in the actual performance of specific routines (see Wright,

2016, for a proposal for a communicative, embodied constitution of organizational routines).

The purpose of the following analysis is to show how the participants sustain power relations between them by (dis)orienting to a specific organizational routine. The analysis applies a multimodal, conversation analytical approach (Sacks, Schegloff, & Jefferson, 1974; Sidnell & Stivers, 2013; Stivers & Sidnell, 2005) by building specifically upon the fundamental conversation analytical concepts of adjacency pairs (Sacks et al., 1974) and preference (Schegloff, Jefferson, & Sacks, 1977) and, in line with recent developments within conversation analysis, by applying a multimodal perspective (Stivers & Sidnell, 2005). This implies that, apart from the detailed analysis of the verbal interaction, the multimodal sequential environment (facial expressions, gesture, body posture, and multiple participants—press and clerks—and material environment) is included in the analysis. This broader analytical perspective enables us to take into account the full array of verbal, embodied, and material resources that participants have at their disposal when negotiating power in organizational routines.

In the video clip, the marriage-certificate issuance can be defined as an organizational routine in which a formalized organizational interaction between citizen and county clerk shapes, (re)confirms, and re-evaluates their power relations. For our analysis, we have chosen an extract of the video (ll. 74–78, re-transcribed below) where the county clerk tries to make the clients and the press leave the room.

The overall argumentation for the micro-level analysis is that power tensions arise by means of the participants either orienting or disorienting to the routinized nature of the interaction. We show this by focusing on five lines of the original transcript, which we revised in order to allow for a multimodal conversation analysis with its focus on microanalysis of social interaction. While the clerk in these lines orients to and thereby sustains the routinized nature of the interaction by demonstrating her entitlement to decide upon the presence of the clients and the press, the client tries to short-circuit the routinized nature of the interaction by making personal matters relevant next actions.

Below, the lines in focus (50–53 in original transcription), where the county clerk tries to make the client and the press leave the room, are re-transcribed according to conversation analytical transcription conventions (Jefferson, 2004), and clips of the interaction are included in order to support the multimodal orientation of the participants.

1 MOORE: [.HH What's the longest you've been with someone,
        [(((CL1, Davis, McKinney look at Moore, Davis nods slightly repeatedly))
        [(((CL2 works at desk, looks down at desk))
        [(((Moore looks at Davis; Ermold looks at Davis))
        [(((Moore positions l. arm over r. arm on counter))

Figure 3.2 Line 1

2   MOORE: [that y<u>ou</u>'ve been married to s<u>o</u>me[one?
                    [((CL1, Davis, McKinney look at Moore))
                    [((CL2 works at desk, looks down at desk))
                    [((Moore looks at Davis, Moore's l. arm over r. arm on counter))
3   PRESS: [((laughter))
4   DAVIS: [.mt I'm <u>a</u>sking you to [l<u>ea</u>ve.=((soft voice))
                    [((Davis, McKinney look at Moore))
                    [((CL1 narrows head a bit, still orienting to D))
                    [((CL2 works at desk, looks down at desk))
                    [((Moore looks at Davis))
                                            [((Davis moves forward with upper body and nods))

Figure 3.3 Line 4

5 MOORE: =[I'm n<u>o</u>t leaving;
          [(((CL1, Davis, McKinney look at Moore))
          [(((CL2 works at desk, looks down at desk))
          [((Moore looks at Davis, Moore's l. arm over r. arm on counter))

Figure 3.4 Line 5

6 (0.3)   ((CL1, Davis, McKinney look at Moore, CL2 works at desk,
              looks down at desk, Moore looks at Davis, Moore's l. arm
              over r. arm on counter))

In lines 1 to 2 (*What's the longest you've been with someone, that you've been married to someone?*), the client Moore ends his multi-unit turn by posing a request for information in the form of a question to the clerk, Davis, including eye contact. By this information request he does not address routine-relevant aspects but instead points to private social aspects related to the clerk, which is not part of the ordinary routine practice of issuing marriage licenses.

Davis responds (l. 4) by strictly remaining within the institutionalized organizational routine of a client-clerk relationship. She ignores the first pair part produced by Ermold by providing a non-type-conform second pair part in the form of a request in line 4 (*I'm asking you to leave*). She does so in a preferred way without any delay, restarts, or repairs; she uses a soft voice, smiles, and nods while moving her upper body towards Ermold. That way, Davis displays strong entitlement to decide upon what are legitimate next actions in this organizational setting and thereby aiming to accomplish a legitimacy to not respond to the question raised by Ermold.

It is noteworthy that it is not Davis alone who orients to and makes the routinized nature of the interaction relevant, but all the rest of the clerks contribute to that. This is accomplished by the way the clerks are positioned (calmly observing for clerk 1 and continuing their ordinary desk work for clerk 2) throughout the analyzed sequence, thereby indicating that they do not treat the ongoing interaction as in any way outside ordinary routine practices. The whole setup is very much out of the ordinary; however, by undauntedly continuing the performance of their regular tasks the clerks preserve a sense of routine "normality" on their side of the counter, which also legitimizes Davis's insistence on maintaining a normal client-clerk interaction.

In line 5, Ermold responds by producing a type-conform, though dispreferred, response to the clerk's request. He rejects her request (*I am not leaving*), but by responding in a type-conform way, the client gives up on his prior action in lines 1 and 2 to which he has not yet received any answer. Instead, he now formally and content-wise responds to a competing action that the clerk has made relevant. That way, it is the clerk's orientation to the routinized nature of the interaction that sets the scene for next relevant actions to come.

This short exemplary analysis contributes to an empirically grounded understanding of how aspects of power and authority come into play and serve as an interactional resource in the creation and maintenance of organizational routines. Through the analysis we show how power is dynamic, emergent, and up for negotiation during the in-situ performance of the organizational routine interaction and that power serves as an interactional resource available to the co-participants in the accomplishment and negotiation of routine relevant actions. We argue that the application of a multimodal conversation analysis approach is an adequate method when studying phenomena such as authority, power, and routines since, by its micro-level focus, it enables us to show the sequential details of the social interaction. The above analysis clearly indicates that the phenomenon of power is intersubjective in nature and that the maintenance of organizational routines seems to be deeply grounded not in the individual organizational member but instead in the multimodal *inter*action between the routine participants. Hence, detailed conversation analytical studies assist us in forming the grounds for a deeper understanding of the relations between routine practices and the enactment of power and authority.

Extending Accountability to Scholarly Authority

Klaus Krippendorff

One lesson learned from the careful reading of this transcript is that authority is interactively, consensually, and hence socially co-constructed.

Its enactment requires cooperation (Goodwin, 2018) but may also be denied or reversed. Scientific authority is no exception. Natural scientists tend to derive their authority by claiming privileged access to an observer-independent reality that cannot speak and much less be held accountable for supposedly adjudicating the truths of scientific theories. Social scientists who take the interactive use of language seriously cannot defer their agency to what they claim to describe. Instead, they have to accept accountability for the consequences of their own publications entering the very social interactions they described (see Figure 3.5.)

For example, theorists who adopt causal power metaphors from physics in explanations of social phenomena ought to be held accountable for rendering challenges of authorities inconceivable—except by violence (Krippendorff, 1991). Claims that linguistic abstractions—concepts, resources, hierarchical structures, and systems of beliefs, including gods— could propel someone to act against their will effectively discourages critical examination of their discursively constructed nature and amounts to what Gregory Bateson (2000, p. 494) called epistemological pathologies.

Unlike conventional social theorists, as scholars of social interactions, we have to demonstrate awareness of our involvement and provide accounts of social phenomena that encourage the possibility of being challenged by those affected. It suggests avoiding the proposition of theories of social phenomena in terms of conceptions of power as an

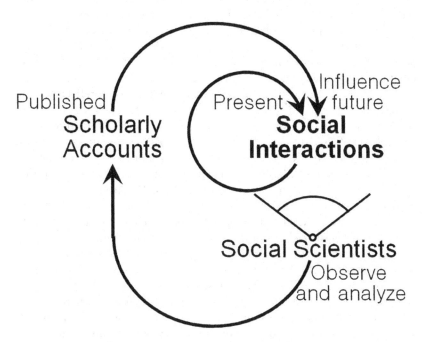

Figure 3.5 Two Levels of Participation in Social Interactions

inevitable force independent of our interpretations (Krippendorff, 1991) and objectifications of message contents which deny readers the ability to interactively establish what texts mean for them (Krippendorff, 2017, 2019). We cannot afford confusing causality and agency, as Latour (2005) does in his Actor-Network-Theory; insisting on discourse as a regime that determines how we think and act, as Foucault proposes (Hall, 2001); or describing human behavior algorithmically, as is the declared aim of artificial intelligence. Such accounts of social phenomena construct unchallengeable social realities that encourage compliance and discourage the interactive evolution of mutually viable alternatives—just in the self-service of scientific authority. For critical scholars, accountability begins by examining what prevents published scholarly constructions of social reality from being challenged.

Discussion

No matter how we look at the organizational phenomena at play, that is, routines, procedures, and authority, it is clear that they are constitutive of and thus central for organizing. Nonetheless, these said-to-be structures are most certainly not fixed. Actors in situations can, to a certain extent, challenge, contest, and negotiate their authorities. Whether we choose to put the emphasis on discourse, materiality, or social accountability, it is possible to highlight as well as to account for the ongoing, multimodal, and relational ways in which many authorities are translated and materialized through situated interactions. What happens during mundane situations where procedures and routines are at play matters to actors as well as to analysts as they represent the very scene where authorities and power can be talked about and where it is possible to witness the somewhat messy character of organizing.

Taking a constitutive lens on organizing enables us to reflect on how the micro-, meso-, and macro-aspects of social life (such as local interactional moves, larger organizational phenomena, and institutions) are interrelated. While much theory still suggests scaling up and scaling down (e.g., Putnam & Nicotera, 2009), indicating that it is possible to distinguish between different organizational layers, the above empirical approaches indicate that this distinction might be questionable. In line with Boden, who pointed out that "the world is of a piece, single and whole . . . there is no such a thing as 'micro' and 'macro'" (Boden 1994, p. 5), the four approaches question such a division into layers.

This again echoes an ethnomethodological concern as raised by Schegloff, who states that "[a] culture is not then to be found only by aggregating all of its venues; it is substantially present in each of its venues" (Schegloff in Sacks, 1992, p. xvii). Consequently, we propose that the micro and the macro are two sides of the same coin, and the question about the micro-macro relationship should be transferred into a question about whose concern is the micro-macro distinction actually. As the empirical studies indicate that the participants do not orient to this distinction, it should not be treated as a member's concern. Instead, if we as analysts keep on dealing with this distinction, it should be kept in mind that we then look at the micro-macro divide as an analyst's construct and concern only. By raising this concern, the above analytical approaches help us shed light on the intersubjective, emergent, and locally situated nature of organizing. Consequently, each of them highlights the relevancy of the researcher's careful positioning towards the data and the phenomenon in focus.

What Do We Learn From Comparing Our Perspectives?

In our five analytical approaches we share much more than we differ in perspectives and methods. We would all agree on working from the ground up, on attending to the sequence of moves and stances taken by interactants rather than simply invoking a structural explanation like rhetoricians or critical theorists might, e.g., of homophobia or heteronormativity. The events at the county clerk's office can be seen from the critical lens of homophobia or heteronormativity, but our interests are in how these conditions are made relevant or contested in and through the interaction. We now see how our approaches not only share commonalities but also each bring light to different facets of authority and power in interactions. Working with five different analytical approaches can be challenging at first, but it is also an opportunity to provide a much richer analysis of one specific interaction.

While we all worked from the ground up, we each brought to bear our favored perspectives to analyze the interaction. The discursive practices of accounting seem central to understanding the argument that composes the transcript. Ventriloquism brings in the different voices that are invoked or used to challenge authority, and it allows us to see that these voices of the courts or of God are ventriloquized in order to account. A multimodal analysis is now widely recognized as a preferred method since it can capture the role of embodiment and physical context, as well as language use, for the emergence and negotiation of power and authority in interaction.

When learning from the different perspectives presented in this chapter, it became clear to us how important it is to keep in mind the strengths of each perspective while at the same time being critically reflexive about their limitations. The way we choose to analyze the data (a ventriloquial, accountability, or micro-level, multimodal routine perspective) has consequences for what we see in the data and what questions we can address. Thus, it is central for the research process to be aware of what you want to focus on, and how you choose to study the phenomenon at stake is consequential for how you understand the emergence of authority and power in interaction.

Table 3.1 Summary of Analytical Approaches to Institutional Authority and to the Routine Exertion of Power

Perspective	Ventriloquial Geneviève Boivin	Accountability Richard Buttny	Critical accountability Klaus Krippendorff	Multimodal routines Helle Kryger Aggerholm and Birte Asmuß	Self-critical Scholarship Klaus Krippendorff
Analytical focus	Ventriloquial analysis of authority in interaction	Discursive analysis of social accountability practices	Communicative agency and accountability for subsequent social constructions of realities	Multimodal conversation analysis of organizational routines	The effects of socially relevant scholarship like the analyses in this book
How authority is constituted in interaction	By mobilizing and challenging the authority of figures	Through pre-existing social positions and how these are supported, challenged, or changed through interaction	By attribution claims derived from being part of an inescapable social organization and subsequent compliance with those attributions	By making use of or deviating from organizational routines	By hiding the scientist's actions behind the claim of finding or consensually establishing theories
How it shifts understanding of authority	Focus on the negotiated nature of authority	Focus on authority as action	Focus on accepting or challenging claims of authorized directives	Authority as a multimodal, interactive accomplishment	By acknowledging that research enters the practices of its stakeholders and becomes either self-fulfilling or encouraging opposition and active invalidation
Key concepts	Figures, ventriloquism, interaction, authorship	Social accountability, accounts, justification, legitimation	Agency; accountability; ability to assume, to comply with, or to challenge authority	Adjacency pairs, entitlement, multimodality, interaction	Reflexive involvement of social scientists in constructing their own subject matter. Active avoidance of abstract and objective claims that make accountability difficult.
Suggested readings	Cooren, F. (2010).	Buttny, R. (2014). Buttny, R., & Morris, G.H. (2001).	Shotter, J. (1984). Mills, C. W. (1940). Krippendorff, K. (1991).	Aggerholm, H.K. & Asmuß, B. (2016).	Krippendorff, K. (2009), especially pp. 86–97.

Hence, working on this chapter was an exercise in appreciating the multi-dimensional nature of social interaction. The introduction to this chapter enumerated what we came to believe we shared: a deep commitment to where and how social phenomena are embodied and practiced. First, Boivin's looking for how we are ventriloquized by the voices of others questions who we really are. Second, Buttny tells us how authority is communicated. Third, as a critical scholar, Krippendorff argues that the exertion of authority implies submission. Holding authorities accountable can disrupt routine exertions of power and create spaces of possibilities that are normatively denied. He also links human agency to such socially constructed spaces which are continuously established as real. Aggerholm and Asmuß's emphasis on routine practices of authority in organizations highlights what we mindlessly do by playing our roles in various organizations. All in all, the encounter we examined demonstrated how routines can be shaken and the claim to be a mere puppet of someone or something else can be questioned, encouraging us to become aware of what we can do. Finally, in view of our analyses of how authority and power are negotiated, Krippendorff reminds us that we cannot escape issues of scientific authority. Not only do we have to provide accounts of our scholarship to our academic communities, we are also accountable to those we theorize, who benefit or may be harmed by our analyses, and to be consistent with our concerns, we also have to refrain from employing explanatory frameworks that leave those described no choice but to comply.

References and Further Readings

Aggerholm, H. K., & Asmuß, B. (2016). When "good" is not good enough: Power dynamics and performative aspects of organizational routines. In J. Howard-Grenville, C. Rerup, A. Langley, & H. Tsoukas (Eds.), *Perspectives on process organization studies* (pp. 140–178). Oxford: Oxford University Press.

Bateson, G. (2000). *Steps to an ecology of mind*. Chicago, IL: University of Chicago Press.

Boden, D. (1994). *The business of talk: Organizations in action*. Cambridge: Polity Press.

Buttny, R. (1993). *Social accountability in communication*. London: Sage.

Buttny, R. (2014). Accounting research. In W. Donsbach (Ed.), *The concise encyclopedia of communication*. Oxford: Blackwell Publishing Ltd.

Buttny, R., & Morris, G. H. (2001). Accounting. In W. P. Robinson & H. Giles (Eds.), *The new handbook on language and social psychology* (pp. 285–302). New York: John Wiley & Sons.

Cooren, F. (2010). *Action and agency in dialogue: Passion, incarnation and ventriloquism*. Philadelphia: John Benjamins Publishing.

Cooren, F. (2012). Communication theory at the center: Ventriloquism and the communicative constitution of reality. *Journal of Communication, 62*(1), 1–20.

Dionysiou, D. D., & Tsoukas, H. (2013). Understanding the (re)creation of routines from within: A symbolic interactionist perspective. *Academy of Management Review, 38*(2), 181–205.

Feldman, M. S. (2000). Organizational routines as a source of continuous change. *Organization Science, 11,* 611–629.

Feldman, M. S., & Pentland, B. T. (2003). Reconceptualizing organizational routines as a source of flexibility and change. *Administrative Science Quarterly, 48*(1), 94–118.

Goodwin, C. (2018). *Co-operative action.* New York: Cambridge University Press.

Hall, S. (2001). Foucault: Power, knowledge and discourse. In M. Wetherell, S. Taylor, & S. J. Yates (Eds.), *Discourse theory and practice, a reader* (pp. 72–81). Thousand Oaks, CA: Sage.

Jefferson, G. (2004). Glossary of transcript symbols with an introduction. In G. H. Lerner (Ed.), *Conversation analysis: Studies from the first generation* (pp. 13–31). Amsterdam: John Benjamins.

Krippendorff, K. (1991). The power of communication and the communication of power; Toward an emancipatory theory of communication. *Communication, 12,* 175–196.

Krippendorff, K. (2009). *On communicating, otherness, meaning, and information.* New York: Routledge.

Krippendorff, K. (2017). Three concepts to retire. *Annals of the International Communication Association, 41*(1), 92–99. doi: 10.1080/23808985.2017.1291281

Krippendorff, K. (2019). *Content analysis: An introduction to its methodology* (4th edition). Thousand Oaks, CA: Sage.

Lammers, J. C., & Barbour, J. B. (2006). An institutional theory of organizational communication. *Communication Theory, 16*(3), 356–377.

Latour, B. (2005). *Reassembling the social: An introduction to actor-network-theory.* Oxford: Oxford University Press.

LeBaron, C. (2008). Microethnography. In K. Tracy (Ed.), *The international encyclopedia of communication.* Cambridge: Blackwell.

Mills, C. W. (1940). Situated actions and vocabularies of motive. *American Sociological Review, 5*(1), 904–913.

Putnam, L. L., & Nicotera, A. M. (2009). *Building theories of organization: The constitutive role of communication.* New York: Routledge.

Sacks, H. (1992). *Lectures on conversation.* Oxford: Blackwell.

Sacks, H., Schegloff, E. A., & Jefferson, G. (1974). A simplest systematics for the organization of turn-taking for conversation. *Language, 50*(4), 696–735.

Schegloff, E. A., Jefferson, G., & Sacks, H. (1977). The preference for self correction in the organization of repair in conversation. *Language, 53*(2), 361–382.

Scott, M. B., & Lyman, S. M. (1968). Accounts. *American Sociological Review, 33*(1), 46–62.

Shotter, J. (1984). *Social accountability and selfhood.* Oxford: Basil Blackwell.

Sidnell, J., & Stivers, T. (Eds.). (2013). *The handbook of conversation analysis.* Cambridge: Wiley-Blackwell.

Stivers, T., & Sidnell, J. (2005). Introduction: Multimodal interaction. *Semiotica, 156,* 1–20.

Wright, A. (2016). Organizational routines as embodied performatives: A communication as constitutive of organization perspective. *Organization, 23*(2), 147–163.

4   Bodies, Faces, Physical Spaces and the Materializations of Authority

Nicolas Bencherki, Alaric Bourgoin, Huey-Rong Chen, François Cooren, Vincent Denault and Pierrich Plusquellec

There is an increasing interest in the language and social interaction community for the bodily and material elements that participate in interaction (Brassac, Fixmer, Mondada, & Vinck, 2008; Nevile, Haddington, Heinemann, & Rauniomaa, 2014). This interest has taken the form, among others, of multimodal analysis, which has allowed for drawing attention to the way people position their bodies relative to each other in public space or use pointing to coordinate interaction (Mondada, 2007, 2009), how they orient to and learn about bodies (Koschmann & Zemel, 2011; Zemel & Koschmann, 2016), or how they may bring objects into the interaction (Hindmarsh & Heath, 2003). Documents, presentation slides, photographs, and other artefacts all play a part in animating people, in guiding and displacing action, and in providing durability to otherwise ephemeral conversations (Cooren & Bencherki, 2010; Cooren & Matte, 2010; Vásquez, 2016).

However, interactional studies into bodily and material elements have yet to explore their role in authority and power issues. Other research traditions have hinted at the importance they play, including Foucault's (1977/1995) description of prison design's part in discipline and surveillance, Althusser's (1971) insistence that ideology exists through apparatuses—the Church, the school, a petition—and practices, or more recently Latour's (1992) account of how technology inscribes and provides potency to morality and norms. Each in their own way, these authors have understood that authority and power need to *materialize* in order to *matter*, i.e., to make a difference in any particular situation. They respectively insist on the quite real participation of architecture in controlling prisoners, of the unfolding of a Mass in reproducing ecclesiastic power, or of a seat belt that automatically positions itself on the driver's chest in propagating a particular understanding of drivers as irresponsible. However, they do not quite provide a methodology to tease out such participation in everyday interactions.

This chapter therefore proposes to discuss the ways in which it is possible to observe the kind of difference bodies, spaces, and other physical aspects make in interaction and how that difference can be described in terms of power and authority. The three positions that will be presented here will operate three different sorts of decentering away from human subjects. The first, presented by Vincent Denault and Pierrich Plusquellec, will consist in considering the human body not only as a subject but also as the object of analysis and reflect on ways in which experimental research on nonverbal communication may complete observation of naturally occurring interaction. The second, presented by Nicolas Bencherki and Alaric Bourgoin, will propose a decentering of analysis towards objects and suggest that it is possible to describe them as communicating without reducing them to tools that are only relevant when they are used by human individuals. Finally, a last perspective, presented by François Cooren and Huey-Rong Chen, will bridge the gap between verbal and non-verbal and propose a ventriloquial analysis that embraces the confusion between human and non-human participants rather than seeking to neatly sort them out.

But first, given that we focus on dimensions of the interaction that are not entirely captured by the transcription, we provide below an alternative description of the sequence focusing on the physical setting in which it takes place as well as the nonverbal aspects of what is happening. This description will be then followed by the presentation of the three analytical positions.

Description of the Interaction

A service counter divides the frame in two. On the right side, from the viewer's perspective, a mass of people is pressed against the counter, among which several are holding what appears to be video cameras. On the first plane, two men. David Moore wears a black shirt and leans on the counter, his hands joined. The other wears a white shirt and glasses and has one hand flat on the counter—it is David Ermold. On the other side of the counter, two clerks are sitting, one in the first plane and the other further up the counter. The two are separated by a table on which lies a printer. At the back of the main room, several doors seem to lead to individual offices. One of these doors, on the left, is open.

A woman—Kim Davis—emerges from there, wearing a pale blue shirt under a darker blue overall dress. She is followed by Flavis McKinney, a 72-year-old retiree "who came in almost daily to make sure [she] was okay" (Davis, 2018, p. 68) and who will remain next to the door for most of the sequence. As soon as she exits her office and has taken only a few steps towards the clerk in the first plane, Ermold yells at her, "Don't smile at me," while Ermold verbally marks her arrival in saying, "Here she is." She answers, "I did not smile," before taking her place right next to the first clerk and in front of Moore, seeming to rest both her hands on the counter. She then explains that she is not being disrespectful to them, which the two men deny.

As they speak, camera shutters can be heard. One cameraman lifts his camera up to take a high-angle shot over people's heads. While the two men remain still while talking, Davis has her head slightly tilted and makes small hand gestures. For instance, when she is asked whether she "would do this to an interracial couple," she answers, "A man and a woman, no," which she accompanies with a sideways gesture of the right hand. Both she and Moore bob their heads as they keep talking, but she is more expressive, as when she makes a broad pointing gesture towards the crowd when she says, "I would ask you all," or when she points at herself and then to Moore when preparing to say, "I've asked you all to leave," and then makes a sideways gesture with both hands as she mentions that people are interrupting her business and no marriage licenses would be issued that day. Moore then asks her why she is not issuing licenses and, following her dry answer—she tilts her body forward and says "Because (.) I'm not"—Ermold clarifies: "Under whose authority?" The question seems to surprise Davis, who turns her body to the right towards Ermold, frowns slightly in what may appear as a defiant look, and answers slowly "Under God's authority."

At that point, McKinney, the retiree who had remained at the back, begins moving toward the front of the room. Camera shutters continue to roar, telephones are taken out to record, and journalists' video cameras continue to turn. The clerk in the front plane remains remarkably still, and her colleague appears to focus on his reading. Some moments later, Moore raises his voice and points accusingly at Davis as he reminds her that he pays her salary. When he says, "I'm paying you to discriminate against me right now, that's what I'm paying for," he bangs his fist on the table a few times. He then points at Ermold, and then slaps his hand on the counter when he says, "I'm paying (.) for this memory (.) with my partner that I love and that I've been with for seventeen years." He then slightly bends forward toward Davis when he asks her, "What's the longest you've been with someone, that you've been married to someone?" This is when she invites people to "push back" away from the counter and makes a gesture as if she were guiding the crowd backwards—to no avail.

When Moore tells her that they are not leaving until they have a license, Davis turns around, makes a dismissive sign behind her, as if to indicate she is ignoring the men, and walks back to her office. As she is about to enter, Moore forcefully and accusatively points at her and yells, "Call the police." The woman waves one last time and enters her office. The first-plane clerk keeps looking at Moore the whole time, and her colleague continues to read something. We also see McKinney slightly approaching Davis's office. The cameras, after having followed Davis, turn back to Moore.

Moore then yells that "everyone in this office should be ashamed of themselves," which prompts Ermold to put his hand on Moore's shoulder.

He points somewhere—perhaps at McKinney—as he asks, "Is this what you want to remember? Is this what you want to remember, that you stood up for this?" McKinney answers at that point, "Amen, yes sir." Moore begins to bang his fist on the table, as he continues, "That your children will have to look at you and realize that you are bigots, and that you discriminated against people?" McKinney then answers, "No, no discrimination," at which point Davis comes out again from her office. As McKinney explains that he finds solace in God's words, and as Moore tilts his body forward to explain that "God does not belong in the county clerk's office," Davis walks back to her previous position in front of Moore and next to the first clerk. When she arrives, Moore slaps his left hand on the counter and repeats—speaking of the police—"Somebody call them."

As the two sides continue to argue, Davis continues to make hand gestures while Moore bends towards her, his hands joined on the counter, and while Ermold looks at her, his right hand on the counter. Cameras continue to record, shutters continue to shut, and the first clerk looks at them while the other hands a sheet over the counter to someone, which seems to indicate he is attending to a client. He then looks briefly towards Davis. From the far right of the room, behind the two men, someone screams at Davis, "This is not the house of God! . . . Do your job . . . But you're forcing your religion on other people." This screaming from behind him appears to break Moore's concentration, as he turns around towards the crowd and asks, "Can you guys shut up?" After a brief pause, Moore explains himself: "You're the press, so shut up."

The people at the back then clarify that they are also waiting for a marriage license, a clarification that is followed by an apology, a brief laughter, all the cameras turning towards the newly discovered allies, and an invitation by Moore to come to the front. Meanwhile, on the other side of the counter, another man, in a white shirt, emerges from a door at the back of the room to speak with McKinney, who then follows him to the back while a journalist in a turquoise shirt manages to get to the front of the pack and to put his microphone on the counter. When the two partners finally position themselves next to Moore, they explain to Davis that she should resign, as she looks intently at them before mimicking taking a hat off and explaining that she cannot separate her beliefs from herself. Ermold then says she should quit, and Davis turns towards him with a surprised but defiant look and asks, "Why should I do that?" In the meantime, the second clerk reaches out for a sheet of paper behind him.

After the brief discussion between Davis and the two men over quitting, the first clerk now has her hands positioned as a triangle in front of her and seems to be waiting this situation out. The second clerk continues to look at whatever he is reading. Shutters continue to be heard, and camera people continue filming. Davis points at herself, saying that she is ready to face her consequences, and then points at the two men, notifying them that they will also face theirs "when it comes time for judgment," displaying what appears like a look of displeasure. She points at them again to indicate that it is their choice not to believe after they tell her they don't. When the conversation moves to whether she made herself the "figurehead of this new church," Davis leans towards the two men and seems to count on her hands as she explains that "Jesus is the same today, yesterday, and forever." This seems to upset Moore, who points at himself and then looks at Ermold, before asking Davis, "Do you even know what our religious beliefs are?" He then makes several hand gestures as he answers himself, "You know why? You don't need to know, we don't need to know yours." He goes further and taps into his hand and says that he believes she "should have the right to have whatever beliefs [she] want[s]."

At that point, she points a complicit finger at Moore and repeats "exactly" several times. Davis then highlights, with a circling motion of the hands, that the two couples can get a marriage license in any surrounding county, an argument that is dismissed by Moore, who insists that they do not have to do so since it is legal in their county. At that point, the second clerk reaches out for another sheet of paper behind him. Moore then states that it may take five years to sue her, which he does not want to do, and Davis seems to concur by pointing first at Moore and then to herself, saying that she does not want them or her to be "put out any more than that." She then raises her finger up and proclaims that there is a remedy, which would consist in the governor of the state doing his job.

Having described some—although certainly not all—nonverbal aspects of the sequence, we now present three different ways to analyze the materialization of authority. While the first section, authored by Vincent Denault and Pierrich Plusquellec, focuses on experimental research on facial expressions and gestures as well as other bodily elements, including proxemics, to inform conversation analysis, the second section, authored by Nicolas Bencherki and Alaric Bourgoin, mobilizes a transductive approach to analyze how the action of physical and architectural elements take their significance and meaning from their participation to broader systems of action. Finally, François Cooren and Huey-Rong Chen present a ventriloquial analysis of this sequence by focusing on how two opposite situations end up materializing themselves in these circumstances.

An Experimental Research Approach

Vincent Denault and Pierrich Plusquellec

According to Stivers and Sidnell (2005), "face-to-face interaction is, by definition, multimodal interaction in which participants encounter a steady stream of meaningful facial expressions, gestures, body postures, head movements, words, grammatical constructions, and prosodic contours" (p. 2). Unfortunately, even if particular bodily actions such as gaze direction, facial expression and body orientation are studied by conversation analysts (e.g., Goodwin, 1980; Kaukomaa, Peräkylä, & Ruusuvuori, 2015; Mondada, 2009), transcriptions often lack visuospatial modalities that would otherwise help "to obtain a more complete understanding of the dynamic nature of the conversation that is unfolding in real time" (Ashenfelter, 2007, p. 3).

Moreover, even if nonverbal communication has been the subject of thousands of peer-reviewed publications since the 1960s (see Plusquellec & Denault, 2018), exchanges between these traditions, often adopting experimental approaches, and conversation analysts remain rare. However, regardless of epistemological and methodological differences that may seem irreconcilable, such a rich body of knowledge "can lead to novel insights into language and social interaction" (Kendrick, 2017, p. 9). Experimental research on facial expressions and proxemics may be of great relevance to understand power and authority issues in interaction, what Judith Hall called the vertical dimension of human relationships (Hall, Coats, & Smith LeBeau, 2005).

Facial expressions, in particular, have received scientific attention at least since the 1860s, when French neurologist Guillaume Duchenne de Boulogne (1862/1990) used electricity to stimulate facial muscles and study emotions. Just a few years later, English naturalist Charles Darwin (1872) wrote on the subject, but scientific attention remained limited until the 1960s when American psychologist Paul Ekman started to study the cross-cultural aspect of nonverbal communication and gave an impetus to research on facial expressions (Ekman, 2003). Among various bodily elements, facial expressions are probably the aspect of nonverbal communication that has come under the closest scrutiny from academics (Plusquellec & Denault, 2018).

For example, using the Facial Action Coding System (FACS; Ekman & Friesen, 1978), a coding system to describe facial-muscle contractions (referred to as Action Units, or AU), several academics consider that different facial expressions reflect different underlying emotional states (Du & Martinez, 2015; Ekman, 2016). According to the neurocultural perspective, facial expressions are similarly displayed by people from different cultures when they experience the same basic emotions. However, social conventions can modify their display to what is more socially appropriate according to the context. Therefore, emotional facial expressions described using the FACS can represent "a combination of one's true feelings and the feelings that one wishes to project" (Burgoon, Guerrero, & Floyd, 2010, p. 302). Understanding the ins and outs of this perspective offers several hints into how Davis's, Moore's, and Ermold's power and authority can be influenced by their emotional facial expressions.

With regards to Davis, from the outset of and throughout the interaction with Ermold and Moore, she displays emotional facial expressions which seem to contradict, confirm, modulate and accentuate (Ekman, 1965) the vocal and verbal modalities of her discourse. At the very beginning, when Davis emerges from her office at the back of the main room, she looks in the direction of Ermold and Moore and displays a smile (what the FACS would code as AU6+AU12), which likely explains Ermold's comment: "Don't smile at me." However, Davis's answer, "I did not smile," comes into contradiction with (or a least modulates) her facial expression, whether or not her smile shows her true feeling or the feeling that she wishes to project. She smiles, but she denies it. While this detail might at first seem anecdotal, similar contradictions can call into question the authority under which she really acts, and more so considering that experimental studies highlighted a relation between the intensity, frequency and duration of a facial expression (including smiling) and power and authority (de Lemus, Spears, & Moya, 2012; Hecht & LaFrance, 1998; Hess, Blairy, & Kleck, 2000; Knutson, 1996).

For example, when Davis is asked under whose authority she acts, she replies: "Under God's authority." However, the facial expression of anger (AU4+AU7+AU31) she displays while replying comes into contradiction with (or at least modulates) the peaceful and respectful tone of her voice (a vocal modality) or the words she used at the very beginning of the interaction (e.g., "I'm not being disrespectful to you"; a verbal modality). A similar contradiction is also displayed when Davis says that she is ready to face the consequences of her actions and that Moore and Ermold will also face theirs "when it comes time for judgment," along with a facial expression of disgust (AU9+AU10) as she looks in their direction.

Therefore, if one was to argue that actions "Under God's authority" ought to be based on love, peace and respect, the contradictions between bodily and spatial—what we term visuospatial—as well as verbal and vocal modalities can call into question the authority under which she acts. Is it really under the authority of a God of love, peace and respect? When, on the contrary, Davis expresses anger and disgust, despite her previous verbal and vocal modalities, one could argue that she now acts under the authority of a different God, namely the God of Judgment Day, a God that tells her not to allow a gay couple to get married, a God that will punish Moore and Ermold, a God that is feeling anger and disgust toward the gay couple, and her negative facial expressions would therefore confirm (or at least accentuate) the authority under which she acts.

Obviously, the use of findings from experimental research on nonverbal communication to understand power and authority issues in interactions exceeds facial expressions. Proxemics, or "the study of our perception and structuring of interpersonal and environmental space" (Harrigan, 2005, p. 137), is another research subject that could be deemed very informative for conversation analysis. As Paul Ekman did for facial expressions, the beginning of research on proxemics dates back to the 1960s and the work of American anthropologist Edward T. Hall, who developed the landmark notation system for interpersonal distances (Hall, 1959, 1963).

Using naturalistic research methods, Hall divided them in four categories: 1) the intimate distance for private and informal interactions, 2) the personal-casual distance for romantic partners, family, friends and coworkers, 3) the social-consultative distance for casual and formal interactions and 4) the public distance for interactions between people of different hierarchy such as speakers with their audiences and celebrities with their fans (Burgoon et al., 2010). However, research on proxemics goes well beyond those four categories. The interaction between Davis, Moore and Ermold appears to be particularly telling on the proxemic norms differentiating superiors from subordinates. For example, compared to the territory of lower status individuals, higher status individuals tend to have larger and less accessible territories (Remland, 1981). They may also have more control over the conversational distance (Dean, Willis, & Hewitt, 1975) as well as the initiation and the interruption of a conversation (Burgoon & Dunbar, 2006; Hall et al., 2005). The physical setting where the interaction between Davis, Ermold and Moore takes place provides a perfect example of such proxemics norms.

Located at the back of the main room, Davis's office is a closed space, rather inaccessible for anyone who comes through the front door of the building. If Moore and Ermold wanted to access Davis's office, they would have to jump over the service counter and kick down a door. Compared to the two clerks' working space, accessible only by leaning over the counter, Davis's office offers greater security from undesirable clients, a visuospatial modality that implies power and authority. Furthermore, such an isolated space, behind walls and the counter, allows Davis to initiate and interrupt the interaction at her own will, which accentuates the power asymmetry with Moore and Ermold. The fact that she has a lot more room to move and decide on the conversational distance when she wants to speak to them also accentuates such power asymmetry. This is further evidenced when, by leaning repeatedly on the counter, Moore arguably appears to call into question the distance created by the counter, as if he were trying to invade as much as possible Davis's privileged space.

Furthermore, since experimental research suggests that louder voices as well as more expressive faces and gestures are perceived to be associated with higher status individuals (Hall et al., 2005), one could also hypothesize that Moore and Ermold embrace such behaviors during their interaction with Davis to communicate power, lower the power asymmetry and try to secure submission to their verbal request (Burgoon & Dunbar, 2006). However, since their strategy fails, one could argue that Davis considers that the power communicated by their behaviors (or by any other sources) did not outweigh the power of the God of Judgment Day.

While experimental research on facial expressions and gestures as well as other bodily elements, including proxemics, also have limitations, the above analysis serves as an example on how considering this body of knowledge could enrich our understanding of power and authority issues in interactions.

A Transductive Approach

Nicolas Bencherki and Alaric Bourgoin

Another way of decentering authority away from the sole contribution of human beings is to look at what *things* do. To avoid bringing back human beings in the picture, we must be able to describe the meaning of those action without resorting to human interpretation. This is key when negotiating authority, as being able to present meaning as stemming from another source besides one's own interpretation can be crucial in shaping a situation to which all parties defer. In other words, being able to say "the computer needs an upgrade" requires the IT technician to fix the computer more compellingly than someone saying "I believe that you should do something."

We propose to call such a perspective, where authority concerns the ability of things to act and the meaning of those actions, "transductive" in the sense that we pay attention to the way action is carried around through people, artefacts and other entities. The term "transduction" was coined by French philosopher Gilbert Simondon (1958/2005) to refer to the way action is transported along a series of entities of various ontologies: for instance, the action of raising a glass takes several consecutive incarnations, from interactions between brain cells processing visual stimuli, to electric current flowing along a nerve, to serotonin crossing a synapse, until it translates into a sequence of coordinated muscle movements. One important theoretical assumption that we make—and that we borrow both from Simondon and from ethnomethodology (Garfinkel, 1967, 1996)—is that what an action or an object means is what it contributes to a broader action. In other words, we consider action to compound yet other actions to which it provides meaning. For instance, what the movement of our arm means can only be understood in the "context" of raising our wine glass, which in turn takes on a particular sense as it contributes to "giving a toast" (a similar idea can be found in the distinction between a wink and a blink in Geertz, 1973).

Simondon's (1958/2005) approach to signification has the advantage of de-personalizing meaning: we do not need people to form a meaning in their minds, and then to share it verbally or in other meaningful actions, for meaning to be observable. In a transductive perspective, people mean things, but so do an arm, a wine glass, or other objects, as long as they contribute it to a more complex system of action that provides them with meaning by forming their context. In this sense, our proposal is close to the way conversation analysis understands the notion of context: it is not of a different analytical level than the communicative actions under study; rather, context is offered by prior and subsequent action inasmuch as together they form an activity in which participants are engaged (Goodwin & Heritage, 1990).

However, a transductive perspective does not limit this view of meaning and context to the actions and activities produced through human language alone. The revolving doors at a building's entrance slow down the flow of people not because they (the doors) *want* to or because people *interpret* them as such but because, as far as the broad activity of people moving in and out of the building, the revolving doors' contribution indeed—and probably without anyone wanting this—consists in slowing down people's flow. There is no need to attribute intention to the revolving doors, or to survey users' understanding, to observe this contribution. As far as other activities may be concerned—say, preventing wind drafts—the revolving doors may contribute other actions and therefore have different meanings.

The fact that the same action (whether it is authored by a human or not) can participate to several activities at once and therefore have several concurrent meanings is, for instance, what Davis, Moore and Ermold discover at the very beginning of the transcript. Davis comes out of her office and moves towards the two men, sporting what appears like a grin. For Moore, this is a "smile," as it is according to the Facial Action Coding System introduced in the previous analysis. He seems to attribute this meaning to the apparent grin because he locates it within the context of a history of tense relationship between Davis and him. For her part, Davis denies this meaning and seems to explain this denial by the fact that "I'm not being disrespectful to you" (line 8). Moore immediately rejects this explanation. He provides a different activity to which the alleged smile contributes and that provides it with its 'disrespectful' meaning: the fact that she is "treating [them] as second-class citizens" (line 10).

In this sense, power or authority is exercised over the meaning of action by pointing out the activity to which it contributes and therefore taking advantage of the fact that action may have several concurrent meanings at once because it contributes to several activities at once. This first example, however, could be reduced to a situation where two people, Davis and Moore, struggle over the meaning of an "object," the so-called smile. Yet, even in this case it should be acknowledged that a physical feature of the situation contributed something to the activity underway independently of human control (unless we suppose Davis intentionally smiled and then lied about it). To borrow from Derrida (1994), we could say that "it smiled" in the same way that "it rains," and that human actors then had to deal with this unexpected action/contribution to the interaction.

Another case will help illustrate the contribution of objects to interaction, and the way they participate to authority, even without obvious controversy over meaning between human participants. It is perhaps the most obvious non-human participant in the interaction between Davis and the two men: the counter (see also the analysis of a service counter in Latour, 1996). The counter *does* two things that appear to be significant in this interaction: it prevents movement from one side of the room to the other, and it offers a surface between the two parties. These two actions may appear to be obvious, but their meaning is revealed to be particularly important when it is looked at through the lens of the activities to which they contribute.

Interestingly, the clerk at the back of the room, away from where Davis, Moore and Ermold are arguing, offers an example of what may perhaps be the more usual contribution of the counter. When a person who appears to be a client approaches the clerk, the counter *separates* the two individuals and *establishes* two distinct spaces in the interaction, that of the clerk, who is sitting and has his equipment and documents accessible to him on his side, some of which—including the computer screen—are hidden from the client, and that of the client, who remains standing up, out of reach from the clerk's material. Power and authority, in this sense, also take the form of the imbalance created by the counter, in terms of access to information and to the tools and documents required to evaluate client requests and grant or deny them.

The counter also offers a delimited collaboration space to both parties to the extent that the countertop constitutes a surface on which the client and the clerk can jointly look at documents, fill them, etc. This is exactly what happens in this case, as the client puts what seems to be a piece of paper on the counter, and both men orient to it. In this sense, the counter not only separates the two sides of the service interaction and defines which of the two parties has control over it but also delineates the extent to which the client can be involved in the processing of his own demand.

Coming back to the first plane of the interaction, Davis herself notes the crucial part played by the counter in the interaction and more generally in the county clerk's office when, at line 80, she asks people to "push back away" from the counter, accompanying the demand with a hand gesture, after noting that they are "interrupting [her] business." This comment by Davis, and the subsequent refusal of people to push back, constitutes a recognition that the very crowding of the room by Moore, Ermold and their supporters constitutes a form of disruption and resistance. This reiterates the central role played by the counter in the service interaction and in the institution of clerks' authority as described above: by preventing access to the counter, resisters are also rendering inoperative the main instrument of administrative authority in Davis's office.

Yet, the counter still contributes to creating an imbalance between the two groups. First, even in this unusual situation, it continues to play its role of establishing two unequal spaces. On the side of the couple, the space (and the screen as we watch the recording) is very crowded, to the point that sight and movement are difficult. For instance, Moore does not see who is shouting behind him and does not at first realize it is a fellow gay couple. When he invites the other two men to the front, it takes them a while to move through the crowd.

The importance of this sequence is highlighted when the couple's space (the crowded side of the counter) is contrasted with that of Davis. In agreement with the previous analysis, we see that she can move freely thanks to the floodgate offered by the counter. She chooses the moment when she moves into the room initially and is then able to retreat to her office and to come back again as she pleases. This is especially important given that Moore, who cannot move with the same freedom, must shout at her when she moves away and as the counter creates distance between the two. To some extent, then, it could be said that Moore's shouting following line 94, when Davis leaves to her office, is at least partly *caused* by the counter, as it creates an imbalance between the two parties' abilities to move and therefore establishes increasing distance between them, forcing Moore to shout in order to be heard by Davis.

The counter also continues to delineate the space available for interaction. While Moore does attempt to bend forward to gain a few inches on Davis, as was already pointed out in this chapter's first analysis, his ability to physically express his "request" is limited to the space afforded by the countertop: he bangs his fist or taps his hand on it to state exasperation (e.g., lines 69, 108 and 222), and the journalists whom he invited and are—literally—on his side can put their microphones or voice recorders on the counter to record the argument. The limited form of involvement made possible by the counter means that Moore only had his hands and the incline of his body to express himself physically, thus making him look either angry—as he banged his fist—or perhaps even aggressive, as he bent forward. In contrast, Davis could move back and forth, retreat, make large hand gestures and so forth, allowing her to appear less impatient throughout the interaction and to retreat when, possibly, she had had too much.

A transductive analysis, therefore, recognizes that the counter—and certainly other artefacts in the situation—contributed action to the broader activity in which Davis, Moore and Ermold (and the others) were involved. This contribution did not only depend on the interpretation people made of it, although on one occasion at least Davis did seem to acknowledge the importance of the counter for her "business." In fact, the counter, while instrumental in what was taking place and in creating an imbalance between its two sides, was nearly never mentioned by the parties. By proposing that action takes its significance and meaning from its participation to a broader system of action, a transductive perspective allows moving the analysis of artefacts to what observably takes place without reducing it to what participants say about objects or to a predefined list of possible roles artefacts may play.

A Ventriloquial Approach

François Cooren and Huey-Rong Chen

We now move to what has come to be known as a "ventriloquial" analysis (Cooren, 2010; Cooren, Matte, Benoit-Barné, & Brummans, 2013). What does it mean to study interaction from a ventriloquial perspective, and what can this type of analysis tell us about the enactment of authority? As we will show, a ventriloquial approach focuses not only on speaking and doing, but also, and maybe especially, on *making one speak* or *making one do something* (*faire parler* or *faire faire*, as we say in French). In their interactions, people indeed keep making figures say things ("figure" is the term ventriloquists sometimes use to talk about their dummies), whether these figures are facts, situations, texts, other persons, organizations or institutions, which often act as a *source of authority* (Cooren, 2010). For instance, if X decides to light a cigarette in a public area, Y can react by pointing him to a no-smoking sign posted on a wall. By signaling this sign, Y is *making the sign say something to X*, which is that the latter should refrain from smoking.

Y could have also said, "Sorry, but you cannot smoke here," which appears less like a ventriloquial move, but even in this case, her reaction consists of implicitly invoking an authority (a law or policy) that allegedly allows her to tell X that he is not authorized to smoke. In other words, ventriloquism, whether we deal with verbal or nonverbal communication, has a lot to do with what ethnomethodology calls *accountability*, that is, the accountable character of people's action. If X came to question Y's injunction, the latter could simply reply, "It is the law!" In that sense, *the law is supposed to speak through* Y when s/he calls upon X's conduct. Ventriloquism, then, is about adding *authors* of what is being done or said, hence the etymological link between *authoring* and *authorizing* (Benoit-Barné & Cooren, 2009; Cooren, 2010; Taylor & Van Every, 2000, 2014).

As we see in these illustrations, another interesting aspect of ventriloquism is that it is *bidirectional*. When Y points X to the no-smoking sign, something very strange happens, as the sign is now signaling X that he should put out his cigarette. In other words, by pointing X to the sign, Y and her finger become intermediaries through which the no-smoking sign can express itself and possibly make a difference as a source of authority. Analyzing an interaction from a ventriloquial perspective thus leads us to decenter our analyses, as human beings do not *necessarily* have to be the center of our observations. *When people interact with each other, they can also be positioned or position themselves as the means, intermediaries or media through which other elements speak.* In other words, human interactants are not only ventriloquists, they are also, whether they like it or not, dummies.

Although some ventriloquial moves can be intentional (like the one that consists of pointing to a non-smoking sign), they do not need to be. As soon as we recognize that human beings are as much ventriloquists as they are dummies, our analyses can highlight all the elements of a situation that can express themselves through what is intentionally or unintentionally done or said. This also means that what expresses itself through someone does not necessarily have to be a source of authority or legitimacy for this person, as some elements can have, on the contrary, *delegitimizing effects*. A good example is what happens at the beginning of the interaction between Davis, Ermold and Moore.

1	ERMOLD	Absolutely ludicrous ((Kim David arrives from her office. She is smiling))
2		(1.0)
3	ERMOLD	Don't smile at [me
4	MOORE	[Here she is
5		(0.5)
6	DAVIS	I did not smile
7		(2.0)
8	DAVIS	I'm not being disrespectful to you ((shaking her head))
9	ERMOLD	You absolu[tely have disrespected us
10	MOORE	[You absolutely are, treating us as second-class citizens=
11	DAVIS	=[No I don't ((shaking her head))
12	MOORE	=[is what you are doing, telling us that we don't deserve the same right rights that
13		you do think that you have
14	DAVIS	I'm saying that [you do-

As Kim Davis arrives with what looks like a smile from her office, we see Ermold enjoining her to stop smiling at him (line 3), an injunction to which Davis responds in saying "I did not smile" (line 6) and then, two seconds later, "I'm not being disrespectful to you," (line 8) while shaking her head. Although Davis first denies having smiled at Ermold on line 6, we can interpret what she says on line 8 as a way to call into question how Ermold might have ventriloquized her conduct so far, that is, what he might have *made it say*, i.e., that she disrespects him. Smiling in the context of a conflictual situation can indeed be interpreted as such to the extent that conflicts normally *call for* some kind of seriousness or gravity, which Davis's smile appears here to contradict.

In terms of authority and legitimacy, we can thus note that in saying "Don't smile at me," Ermold is indirectly telling her that the situation they find themselves in *does not allow* her to smile. Ventriloquism is at stake here to the extent that Ermold *makes Davis's smile say* that she is disrespectful to him, something that Davis understands very well when she explicitly denies that such is the case (line 8). While a smile is supposed to mark, in normal circumstances, a form of respect for the client, it becomes, through Ermold's reaction on line 3, a way to *deny* the conflictual situation they are involved in.

Through her smile, a form of lightness, flippancy or detachment is supposed to express itself, while the situation calls, according to him, for seriousness, severity and gravity.

Reacting to Davis's denial, we then see Moore and Ermold affirming that she has been and is disrespectful to them (lines 9–10). Interestingly, Moore ventriloquizes what for him has been her conduct so far when he says, "You absolutely are, treating us as second-class citizens is what you are doing, telling us that we don't deserve the same right rights that you do think that you have" (lines 10, 12–13). In other words, what she has been doing and saying so far (a sequence that might also include the previous encounters the three of them had before) becomes, through Moore's reaction, not only an act of discrimination (as they are allegedly treated as second-class citizens) but also a denial of their rights as citizens, a ventriloquation that Davis again explicitly and implicitly denies (lines 11 and 14).

Throughout a big part of the interaction, except at specific moments we will go back to, Davis will maintain what could be called the face of a professional county clerk, a face that is supposed to contradict Moore and Ermold's accusations of disrespect. This professionalism starts with her smile (line 1) but can also be identified through the calmness of her voice (e.g., lines 19), a calmness that sometimes is accompanied by firmness when she tells everyone on the other side of the counter that they have to leave (lines 55–56, 77) or push back away (lines 80–81). As Moore gets more and more angry, especially when he bangs his hand against the counter while saying, "I pay you to discriminate against me right now, that's what I'm paying for" (lines 69–70), we see her imperturbably reacting with a look and a hand gesture ventriloquizing that it is too bad for him and that there is nothing she can do about it (line 71).

This verbal and nonverbal conduct is important in terms of authority as it allows her to remain the official voice of the office she is supposed to represent. Acting like a professional who does not lose her temper even when she is facing adversity means that she still embodies the role of the county clerk responding to her clients, angry as they might be. Ventriloquial effects can thus be recognized throughout the whole excerpt, as it is the voice and deeds of a "professional clerk" that will keep being heard and observed through her conduct. In other words, when Davis speaks, it is almost uninterruptedly the professional clerk that we hear and see speaking.

Even when the register of professionalism gives way to a more informal (almost intimate) approach on her part, we still see her remaining calm and unruffled. After Moore has been shouting at all the office employees, accusing them of bigotry (line 122) and discrimination (line 124), Davis comes back a second time from her office and starts addressing him with his first name in a calm and polite tone ("David, listen to me" (line 140); "David, please, [I'm asking you, please listen to me" (line 144)), trying to establish a rapport with him (e.g., "I know you don't care" (line 150); "You believe passionately in wh[at you are doing as I do ((making a circle with her hands))" (lines 156–157)).

Two ventriloquations thus appear to oppose each other in this office. On one side, Moore and Ermold, whose expressions of anger and exasperation are supposed to express their indignation regarding what Davis is doing to them (for instance, Moore says, "You do not understand what you are doing to people" at lines 158–159). In other words, the indignant/outrageous/offensive character of the situation is supposed to express itself through their interventions. On the other side, Davis's calmness, politeness and placidity appears to indirectly deny the way Moore and Ermold materialize and ventriloquize the situation. Through what she says, and especially how she says it, it is as if a certain normality of the situation was expressing itself: *she is still serving clients despite everything that might contradict her reading of the situation.*

Through this calmness/politeness/placidity, one could even see an attempt on Davis's part to express a form of love or care (see chapter 6) with which Moore and Ermold's expressions of anger and exasperation contrast, especially if they are understood as an expression of hatred or at least animosity against Davis (see, for instance, lines 21, 74–76). Moore seems to understand the danger this contrast creates as he responds, "I'm beyond listening to you" (line 141), with a tone of exasperation when she starts addressing him with his first name, as if to calm him down. On line 146, he even says, "I don't- I don't care how polite you are," which Davis cleverly takes up by saying, "I know you don't care" (line 150), which appears to add an additional contrast between someone who is supposed to paradoxically care for her interlocutor (Davis) and someone who does not (Moore).

Visibly aware that this contrast is not to his advantage, Moore then replies, "You're not- This is not polite" (line 152), and then, "I would never do this to someone, what you are doing to us, I would never (.) do to someone" (lines 154–155). After having alluded to the extra-politeness of her interventions (line 146), Moore thus now denies it. While Davis is indeed having a conduct that could be considered respectful and considerate of her interlocutors (which is usually what we mean by politeness), something crucial is missing for Moore and Ermold, that is, the fact that she does not respect their legal right to be issued a marriage license. *Moore therefore attempt to undermine Davis's strategy of normalization, a strategy that amounts to denying the extraordinary character of the situation.*

Although we do not have enough space to develop further our analysis, we would like to go back to two moments where a change of register is taking place, that is, moments where Davis appears to take off the mask of calmness and placidity while still remaining polite. The first moment takes place in response to Ermold, who had just asked her, "Under whose authority? (0.5) are you not issuing licenses?" (line 47). Davis then looks defiantly at him and replies, "Under God's authority." This again happens, although maybe in a milder form, where she tells her interlocutors that her beliefs cannot be separated from her (lines 184–186) and when she calls into question the fact that she should resign: "((Turning towards Ermold and looking at him defiantly)) Why should I have to" (line 188).

In both cases, we note that her calmness gives way to defiance, which could also be interpreted as a change in terms of source of authority. While we saw that calmness and placidity allowed her to remain the official voice of Rowan County, these brief moments of defiance appear to position her as none other than (her version of) the voice of God, a God that will, as she reminds her interlocutors, judge their conduct when times come: "I'm willing to face my consequences and you will all face your consequences when it comes time for judgment" (lines 195–196). A sort of mild polyphony can thus be heard throughout this excerpt. While she manages, for the most part, to remain the voice of the office she is supposed to represent, we see the voice of God expressing itself when times come to defend her faith and convictions.

As we tried to show in this section, ventriloquism is about *what* or *who* expresses itself/himself/herself through what is being said or done; that is, it is about all the different ways by which a situation ends up materializing itself through various elements that are supposed to embody it. Although this approach does not question human beings' incredible capacity to not only make sense of situations but also strategically mobilize some of their aspects, it shows that this sensemaking and strategy precisely amounts to ventriloquizing the world they find themselves in. In conflictual situations, like the one we analyzed here, we saw that these activities of ventriloquation keep contradicting each other, that is, literally and figuratively say different things about what the situation is all about.

From a ventriloquial perspective, a conflict not only marks disagreement between two or more people, it also, and maybe especially, expresses at least two different ways to convey what a situation *calls for*. The game of authority that we analyzed thus consists of multiplying the authors that are supposed to say something about what the situation is or requires, whether it is a look, a smile, a politeness register, what is being explicitly said or even God himself. Did we observe a clerk trying to serve her clients the best way she said she could or a clerk blatantly denying a couple their fundamental rights? As our analysis demonstrates, what we actually observed was the clash between these two cooccurring situations, which kept materializing themselves throughout this altercation.

If authoring is about authorizing, the game of authority is about who or what is allowed to ventriloquize itself/himself/herself in a given situation.

Table 4.1 Summary of Analytical Approaches to Authority's Materiality

Perspective	Experimental research approach Vincent Denault and Pierrich Plusquellec	Transductive approach Nicolas Bencherki and Alaric Bourgoin	Ventriloquial approach François Cooren and Huey-Rong Chen
Analytical focus	Facial expressions and proxemics, especially as they are described in experimental research on nonverbal communication	The contribution of action to broader activities	The sharing of action with figures through invocation
How authority is constituted in interaction	By contradiction, confirmation, modulation and accentuation of vocal and verbal modalities.	Through a struggle over the meaning of action, which corresponds to attributing action to different activities	By presenting oneself as authorized to act in a given way by different figures that make up the situation
How it shifts understanding of authority	Shows that comparisons of the speakers' nonverbal behaviors with stated authority sources reveal what actually drives their actions	Connects authority, action and meaning without privileging human interpretation	Shows that authoring and authorizing have a lot to do with each other. By multiplying the author of a position, we tend to look more authorized to voice it.
Key concepts	Facial Action Coding System (FACS), emotion, vertical dimension of human relationships	Transduction, action, meaning, attribution of action	Ventriloquism, polyphony, figure, authoring
Suggested readings	Knapp, M. L., Hall, J. A., Horgan, T. G. (2014). *Nonverbal communication in human interaction.* Boston: Wadsworth.	Simondon, G. (2016). *On the mode of existence of technical objects.* Minneapolis, MN: Univocal Pub.	Cooren, F. (2010). *Action and agency in dialogue.* Amsterdam/ Philadelphia: John Benjamins.

It is this game of expression that the ventriloquial analysis helps us decipher and analyze.

Conclusion

The three analytical perspectives presented above share a commitment to decenter the analysis towards the "things"—whether physical objects or seemingly abstract entities—that are active in the situation. In Vincent Denault and Pierrich Plusquellec's proposal, insights from experimental research comfort the analyst's recognition of facial expressions, which are then compared to verbal statements and actions from their owner. In that sense, facial expressions may challenge the speakers' other expressive modalities and reveal discrepancies between the authority they invoke and what actually drives them to say what they say or do what they do. Nicolas Bencherki and Alaric Bourgoin, for their part, suggest that things may participate in interaction irrespective of the interpretation people make of them. The meaning of their action proceeds from the contribution they make to broader activities. Since a same action may participate to several activities, it also has several meanings. Negotiating authority, then, consists in pointing out different activities to which action contributes, and therefore its very meaning. Finally, François Cooren and Huey-Rong Chen propose an analytical strategy based on the observation of the way people share the authorship of what they say and do with different figures, which are thus brought into the situation and presented as authorizing those actions, thus sharing their authority with the speaker.

References

Althusser, L. (1971). Ideology and ideological state apparatuses: Notes towards an investigation. In *"Lenin and philosophy" and other essays* (pp. 121–176). New York, NY: Monthly Review Press.

Ashenfelter, K. T. (2007). *Simultaneous analysis of verbal and nonverbal data during conversation: Symmetry and turn-taking.* Notre Dame, IN: University of Notre Dame.

Benoit-Barné, C., & Cooren, F. (2009). The accomplishment of authority through presentification: How authority is distributed among and negotiated by organizational members. *Management Communication Quarterly, 23*(1), 5–31.

Brassac, C., Fixmer, P., Mondada, L., & Vinck, D. (2008). Interweaving objects, gestures, and talk in context. *Mind, Culture, and Activity, 15*(3), 208–233. https://doi.org/10.1080/10749030802186686

Burgoon, J. K., & Dunbar, N. (2006). Nonverbal expressions of dominance and power in human relationships. In V. Manusov & M. L. Patterson (Eds.), *The SAGE Handbook of Nonverbal Communication* (pp. 279–297). Thousand Oaks, CA: Sage.

Burgoon, J. K., Guerrero, L. K., & Floyd, K. (2010). *Nonverbal communication.* Boston: Pearson.

Cooren, F. (2010). *Action and agency in dialogue: Passion, ventriloquism and incarnation.* Amsterdam and Philadelphia: John Benjamins Publishing Company.

Cooren, F., & Bencherki, N. (2010). How things do things with words: Ventriloquism, passion and technology. *Encyclopaideia, Journal of Phenomenology and Education,* (28), 35–61.

Cooren, F., & Matte, F. (2010). For a constitutive pragmatics: Obama, Médecins Sans Frontières and the measuring stick. *Pragmatics and Society, 1*(1), 9–31. https://doi.org/10.1075/ps.1.1.02coo

Cooren, F., Matte, F., Benoit-Barné, C., & Brummans, B. H. J. M. (2013). Communication as Ventriloquism: A grounded-in-action approach to the study of organizational tensions. *Communication Monographs, 80*(3), 255–277. https://doi.org/10.1080/03637751.2013.788255

Darwin, C. (1872). *The expression of emotion in man and animals.* New York: Oxford University Press.

Davis, K. (2018). *Under God's authority: The Kim Davis story.* Orlando, FL: New Revolution Publishers.

de Lemus, S., Spears, R., & Moya, M. (2012). The power of a smile to move you: Complementary submissiveness in women's posture as a function of gender salience and facial expression. *Personality and Social Psychology Bulletin, 31*(11), 1480–1494.

Dean, L. M., Willis, F. N., & Hewitt, J. (1975). Initial interaction distance among individuals equal and unequal in military rank. *Journal of Personality and Social Psychology, 32*(2), 294–299. http://dx.doi.org/10.1037/0022-3514.32.2.294

Derrida, J. (1994). *Specters of Marx: The state of the debt, the work of mourning, and the new international.* New York: Routledge.

Du, S., & Martinez, A. M. (2015). Compound facial expressions of emotion: From basic research to clinical applications. *Dialogues in Clinical Neuroscience, 17*(4), 443–455.

Duchenne de Boulogne, G. (1862/1990). *Mécanisme de la physionomie humaine.* Paris: Jules Renouard.

Ekman, P. (1965). Communication through nonverbal behavior: A source of information about an interpersonal relationship. In S. S. Tomkins & C. E. Izard (Eds.), *Affect, cognition and personality* (pp. 389–442). New York: Springer.

Ekman, P. (2003). *Emotions revealed.* New York: Henry Holt.

Ekman, P. (2016). What scientists who study emotion agree about. *Perspectives on Psychological Science, 11*(1), 31–34. https://doi.org/10.1177/1745691615596992

Ekman, P., & Friesen, W. (1978). *Facial action coding system: A technique for the measurement of facial movement.* Palo Alto, CA: Consulting Psychologists Press.

Foucault, M. (1995). *Discipline and punish: The birth of the prison.* New York: Vintage Books. (Original work published 1977).

Garfinkel, H. (1967). *Studies in ethnomethodology.* Englewood Cliffs, NJ: Prentice-Hall.

Garfinkel, H. (1996). Ethnomethodology's program. *Social Psychology Quarterly, 59*(1), 5–21.

Geertz, C. (1973). Thick description: Toward an interpretive theory of culture. In *The interpretation of cultures: Selected essays* (pp. 3–30). New York, NY: Basic Books.

Goodwin, C. (1980). Restarts, pauses, and the achievement of mutual gaze at turn-beginning. *Sociological Inquiry*, *50*(3–4), 272–302. https://doi.org/10.1111/j.1475-682X.1980.tb00023.x

Goodwin, C., & Heritage, J. (1990). Conversation analysis. *Annual Review of Anthropology*, *19*, 283–307.

Hall, E. T. (1959). *The silent language*. Garden City: Anchor

Hall, E. T. (1963). A system for the notation of proxemic behavior. *American Anthropologist*, *65*(5), 1003–1026. https://doi.org/10.1525/aa.1963.65.5.02a00020

Hall, J. A., Coats, E., & Smith LeBeau, L. (2005). Nonverbal behavior and the vertical dimension of social relations: A meta-analysis. *Psychological Bulletin*, *131*(6), 898–924. https://doi.org/10.1037/0033-2909.131.6.898

Harrigan, J. A. (2005). Proxemics, kinesics, and gaze. In J. A. Harrigan, R. Rosenthal & K. R. Scherer (Eds.), *The new handbook on methods in nonverbal behavior research* (pp. 137–198). Oxford: Oxford University Press.

Hecht, M. A., & LaFrance, M. (1998). License or obligation to smile: The effect of power and sex on amount and type of smiling. *Personality and Social Psychology Bulletin*, *24*(12), 1332–1342. http://dx.doi.org/10.1177/01461672982412007

Hess, U., Blairy, S., & Kleck, R. E. (2000). The influence of facial emotion displays, gender, and ethnicity on judgments of dominance and affiliation. *Journal of Nonverbal Behavior*, *24*(4), 265–283. https://doi.org/10.1023/A:1006623213355

Hindmarsh, J., & Heath, C. (2003). Transcending the object in embodied interaction. In J. Coupland & R. Gwyn (Eds.), *Discourse, the body, and identity* (pp. 43–69). London: Palgrave Macmillan. https://doi.org/10.1057/978140 3918543_3

Kaukomaa, T., Peräkylä, A., & Ruusuvuori, J. (2015). How listeners use facial expression to shift the emotional stance of the speaker's utterance. *Research on Language and Social Interaction*, *48*(3), 319–341. https://doi.org/10.1080/083 51813.2015.1058607

Kendrick, K. H. (2017). Using conversation analysis in the lab. *Research on Language and Social Interaction*, *50*(1), 1–11. https://doi.org/10.1080/08351813. 2017.1267911

Knutson, B. (1996). Facial expressions of emotion influence interpersonal trait inferences. *Journal of Nonverbal Behavior*, *20*(3), 165–182.

Koschmann, T., & Zemel, A. (2011). "So that's the ureter": The informal logic of discovering work. *Ethnographic Studies*, *12*, 31–46.

Latour, B. (1992). Where are the missing masses? The sociology of a few mundane artifacts. In W. E. Bijker & J. Law (Eds.), *Shaping technology/building society: Studies in sociotechnical change* (pp. 225–258). Cambridge, MA: MIT Press.

Latour, B. (1996). On interobjectivity. *Mind, Culture, and Activity*, *3*(4), 228–245. https://doi.org/10.1207/s15327884mca0304_2

Mondada, L. (2007). Multimodal resources for turn-taking: Pointing and the emergence of possible next speakers. *Discourse Studies*, *9*(2), 194–225. https://doi.org/10.1177/1461445607075346

Mondada, L. (2009). Emergent focused interactions in public places: A systematic analysis of the multimodal achievement of a common interactional space. *Journal of Pragmatics*, *41*(10), 1977–1997. https://doi.org/10.1016/j.pragma.2008.09.019

Nevile, M., Haddington, P., Heinemann, T., & Rauniomaa, M. (Eds.). (2014). *Interacting with objects: Language, materiality, and social activity*. Amsterdam and Philadelphia: John Benjamins Publishing Company.

Plusquellec, P., & Denault, V. (2018). The 1000 most cited papers on visible non-verbal behavior: A bibliometric analysis. *Journal of Nonverbal Behavior, 42*(3), 347–377.

Remland, M. (1981). Developing leadership skills in nonverbal communication: A situational perspective. *Journal of Business Communication, 18*, 18–31. https://doi.org/10.1177/002194368101800303

Simondon, G. (2005). *L'individuation à la lumière des notions de forme et d'information*. Grenoble: Jérôme Millon. (Original work published 1958).

Stivers, T., & Sidnell, J. (2005). Introduction: Multimodal interaction. *Semiotica, 156*, 1–20. https://doi.org/10.1515/semi.2005.2005.156.1

Taylor, J. R., & Van Every, E. J. (2000). *The emergent organization. Communication as site and surface*. Mahwah, NJ: Lawrence Erlbaum Associates.

Taylor, J. R., & Van Every, E. J. (2014). *When organization fails: Why authority matters*. New York: Routledge.

Vásquez, C. (2016). A spatial grammar of organising: Studying the communicative constitution of organisational spaces. *Communication Research and Practice, 2*(3), 351–377. https://doi.org/10.1080/22041451.2016.1221686

Zemel, A., & Koschmann, T. (2016). A stitch in time: Instructing temporality in the operating room. *Communication & Medicine, 12*(1), 85–98. https://doi.org/10.1558/cam.v12i1.25988

5   God, Love, and the Apparently Immaterial Sources of Authority

Bertrand Fauré, Thomas Martine,
Trudy Milburn, and Katherine R. Peters

Examining (im)materiality is important for the study of authority because objects in the world (whether physical or linguistic) offer affordances for particular types of action (Aakhus et al., 2011). In Kim Davis's case, the materiality of the sources of authority can be tackled through the way they materialize in the participants' communicative actions (including speech, tone, and visible actions). In this chapter, we focus on God and love because they are seemingly more abstract or immaterial sources of authority. Although one could argue that it may be possible to discuss the materialization of all the sources of authority invoked in this interaction, our choice is to focus on these two. We take four lenses to focus on these aspects and conclude with a discussion that contextualizes God and love in broader strokes.

The four analyses below draw upon differing sets of literature. In the first, Martine uses a constitutive view of communication (Taylor & Cooren, 1997; Cooren, 2012) to show how God and love materialize in this interaction as well as the relative authority they acquire as a result. In the second analysis, Peters draws upon the ethnography of communication as explicated by Hymes (1973, 1974) and Blommaert (2009) to describe the way language is used by participants to speak on behalf of either God or love. In the third, Milburn uses tools from cultural discourse theory (Carbaugh, 2007; Scollo, 2011) to suggest that there are distinct cultural premises mustered by participants that are fundamentally agonistic and, therefore, difficult to reconcile within the interaction. In the fourth, Fauré argues that God and Love are the symmetrical highest sources of authority materialized by each party during the interaction.

Despite employing different methodologies and literatures for our analyses, we agree that it is through discourse that the immaterial can be materialized to bring about real changes of state (such as going from unmarried to married). In the four analyses that follow, we all demonstrate that one who is able to assert and maintain higher or legitimate authority to engage in specific actions can make material, relational differences for all of those present in the interaction.

The Constitutive View of Communication

Thomas Martine

In this section, we adopt a constitutive view of communication (Taylor & Cooren, 1997; Cooren 2012, 2015; Putnam & Nicotera, 2009) to analyze the way God and love materialize in this interaction as well as the relative authority they carry as a result. To adopt this view is to consider that things of the world do not inherently possess their properties but acquire them by relating to one another (Latour, 2013; Barad, 2007). In other words, this means that things (whether they are organizations, plants, humans, technologies, emotions, or atoms) do not exist in and of themselves but constantly come to existence by associating with or *passing through* other things; in short, that they are *communicatively constituted* (Cooren, 2012; Cooren & Sandler, 2014).

In this perspective, materiality is not an inert given but an eventful process: from one situation to the next, things materialize more or less depending on the number of other things that support their existence, that is, allow them to express themselves or make a difference (Martine & Cooren, 2016, Martine, Cooren, & Bartels, 2017). From this relational standpoint, materiality and authority are closely related: the more something materializes in or through other beings, the more weight or authority it carries in the sense that it can be viewed as what connects or unifies these beings. The constitutive view of communication thus allows us to analyze not only how seemingly immaterial beings, such as God and love, materialize in a conversation but also the degree of authority they acquire in it (Benoit-Barné & Cooren, 2009).

Let us start with the way God materializes in this interaction. When David Ermold asks Kim Davis "under whose authority are you not issuing licenses" (line 47), she immediately answers "under God's authority" (line 49). This is a powerful response in terms of authority as it implicitly unifies everything that she might say or do to maintain her refusal under one single voice, God's. This means that for Davis or anyone who might share her view, God is at work in almost everything she does and says in this interaction: it manifests itself (i.e., materializes) every time she states "[she is] not issuing license today" (lines 23, 39, 41, 46), every time she asks her interlocutors to leave (lines 55, 77) or to push back away from the counter (lines 80, 86, 89), and when she bids them "good day" and returns to her office (line 94).

In her case, it also materializes or manifests itself in the way she contradicts or denies the gay couple's requests and accusations; for instance, when she denies that her refusal amounts to disrespect (line 8), discrimination (lines 11, 14), or outright disregard for people's life (lines 193–194) and when she discusses the implications of the Supreme Court's decision (lines 30–34). Indeed, she substantiates her refusal by explaining that "[her] beliefs cannot be separated from [her]" (line 184) in response to the idea that she should resign and when she states that "Jesus is the same today, yesterday and forever" (line 210) in response to the accusation of "creating a religion in this office" (line 202).

If her beliefs cannot be separated from her, then God can also be viewed as manifesting itself in the calm with which she carries herself during all the interaction, even when her interlocutors raise their voices (lines 65, 97, 104–124), slam their hands on the counter (lines 108–124, 136), or appear insensitive to her (for instance, when Moore tells her "I don't care . . . what you feel," lines 143–146). What matters in all these instances is not that Davis wins the argument but only that she remains firm in her resolve to behave according to (what she believes to be) God's voice no matter the situation. By doing so, she gives substance to what could be described as a Christian sacrificial posture.

Thus, God enjoys considerable authority in this interaction to the extent that it can be viewed not only as unifying most everything Davis says and does but also as connecting it to a larger religious context in a coherent way. It is noteworthy that this authority cannot be reduced to any of Davis's actions or statements. It would be a mistake, for instance, to reduce it to the statement "[I am acting] under God's authority" (line 49). While this statement is certainly important to designate God as what unifies her actions, it could, at any moment, be contradicted by what she does or says before or after it (e.g., if she deliberately insulted her interlocutors, which would not sound very Christian). For God's authority to keep materializing, it must be consistently designated as the unifier of Davis's action every step of the way, which seems to be the case here.

This being said, God's authority has obvious limits in this interaction as it works only if one shares the view that homosexuality is a sin and that marriage, whether civil or religious, must be protected from it, a view that is obviously not shared by all.

Let us now turn to the way love materializes in this interaction. Love explicitly appears when David Moore makes the following statement (lines 72–75):

MOORE   that's what I'm paying for. I'm paying↑ (.) for this memory (.)
        with my partner that >I love, that I have been with for seventeen
        years<. ((flapping on the counter this his right hand))

By arguing that Davis's refusal to give them a marriage license is creating a painful memory for him and his partner "that [he] love[s]," David implicitly presents love as materializing in their request to have a marriage license, that is, as being one of the reasons they want to get married. Moreover, by emphasizing that they have been together "for seventeen years," he also implicitly presents love as materializing in the long-lasting nature of their relationship, as being its "glue," so to speak.

It is noteworthy that the argument that love is a central motivation for them to get married could be used to expand the authority of love in this interaction. Indeed, it might be tempting to cast everything that the couple says and does to obtain a marriage license (whether it is recalling the Supreme Court's decision, denouncing discrimination, or manifesting their anger) as being, in the final analysis, a matter of love. However, this is not what Moore and Ermold are doing here. For them, love is only one of the various reasons, along with the Supreme Court's decision or the fight against discrimination, for instance, why they should be granted a marriage license. All these reasons certainly intersect, but one cannot be made to speak on behalf of all the others.

Thus, love certainly carries some weight or authority here as it is supposed to be what has allowed this couple to hold over a long period and obviously what brings them to request a marriage license. However, as opposed to the way God is positioned in Davis's discourse, love is never positioned as the unifying force standing under everything Moore and Ermold do and say in this interaction. For this reason, it is probably fair to say that love carries (for them) far less weight or authority than God (for Kim Davis) when it comes to determining whether or not Davis should provide them with a marriage license.

As shown in this analysis, the relational understanding of materiality that is at the heart of the constitutive view of communication allows us to precisely evaluate the degree of authority that seemingly immaterial beings, such as God and love, acquire in this interaction. Beyond this, the merit of this approach is also to detect that the difference of materiality/authority between these two entities has something to do with the argumentative styles of the interlocutors: while Davis positions everything she does and says under one authority, God's, the two men seem to maintain a certain separation between the various sources of authority they convene. We touch here on important questions about the various ways of producing authority (see Latour, 2013) but ones that go way beyond the scope of this section.

Language-in-Society

Katherine Peters

This section is methodologically based in the ethnography of communication (Hymes, 1973, 1974), a tradition out of linguistic anthropology. The ethnography of communication focuses on interpreting language-in-use and is intended to provide concepts and frameworks to allow for comparison between different ways of speaking or speech communities. As an interpretive program, it has been criticized for not attending to power, politics, or authority (Fiske, 1990, 1991). However, Hymes (1973) argues that ethnographers of communication need to pay attention to "what users have made of [language]" (p. 60) and especially the ways in which users make language bolster a position.

Hymes examines speech, and more broadly communication, as "language-in-society" (Blommaert, 2009, p. 264). This orientation to language "deeply situates language in a web of relations of power, a dynamic of availability and accessibility, a situatedness of single acts vis-à-vis larger social and historical patterns" (p. 264). Language cannot be separated from society or its context. Language, "shaped by its history and patterns of use," can thus be shaped in the interests of a powerful few to bolster their authority (Hymes, 1973, p. 73). Although this concept falls short of a sociomaterial analysis of authority, language-in-society does indicate that one could trace histories and meanings through language to find patterns of power and authority in use. The seemingly "immaterial" sources of authority we examine here, God and love, can thus be traced through patterns of use in U.S. society. The use of God and love in the arguments made in this interaction may carry more or less weight (in other words, lend more or less authority) through their histories and patterns of use.

To approach this interaction and the authority of seemingly "immaterial" sources as language-in-society, I examine twin questions: Who has the availability and accessibility to speak on behalf of God and assert His authority, and to what effect? Who has the availability and accessibility to speak on behalf of love in this interaction and assert its authority, and to what effect?

Who Can Speak for God?

Upon reading the transcript, it is apparent that Davis is one interlocutor who has the availability and accessibility to speak on behalf of God and assert His authority. On line 49 in the excerpt below, she states that she is not issuing licenses "under God's authority."

```
47  ERMOLD   Under [whose authority? (0.5) are you not issuing [licenses?
48  MOORE            [Why
49  DAVIS                                          [Under God's authority
50           ((looking defiantly at David Ermold))
51  OTHER    Did the lawyers tell you-
52  MOORE    [Did God tell you to do this? Did God tell you how to treat us (.) like this?
53  ERMOLD   [I don't believe in your god. I don't believe in your god. I don't believe in
54           your [god
55  DAVIS         [((looking at Moore)) I've asked you all to leave, you are interrupting
56           [my business ((opening her arms))
```

Ermold demands to know under whose authority Davis has chosen not to issue licenses, and God provides a weighty source of authority in U.S. society. In the matter at stake, people who speak out against same-sex marriage tend to use God and invoke his authority to provide evidence for their claims (Tracy & Hughes, 2014). The use of this term invokes a web of relations of power around it, one that allows her to dodge an implied criticism through Ermold's repeated statement in lines 53–54,

"I don't believe in your god." As Tracy and Hughes (2014) find in their work, the use of the term "God," "Christ," or the Bible all connect to conservative Christian values. Among these values is the belief that marriage should only be between one man and one woman, not between same-sex partners. Furthermore, Tracy and Hughes note that those who speak out against same-sex marriage bring up religion as a matter of "personal commitment that required them to express religious beliefs" (p. 317).

Throughout the interaction, Davis continues to strengthen the connection between her and God, thus tightening the authority of God over her actions and what she can and cannot allow. In lines 156–157, Davis recognizes the passion with which she holds her belief:

```
156   DAVIS   =You believe passionately in wh[at you are doing as I do ((making a circle
157            with her hands))
```

Moments later, she states that these beliefs are inseparable from her:

```
184   DAVIS   No my beliefs cannot be separated from me I [cannot take my hat off . . .
```

By drawing this stark delineation that her belief in God is inseparable from her being, she draws a clear line for the rest of the interaction. Now that she has claimed this belief and publicly stated her personal commitment, she stakes a heavy claim within the web of relations of power surrounding it. As with others who have argued against same-sex marriage, she demonstrates the requirement to speak out and act on behalf of her conservative Christian values. Around this claim of personal belief and God's authority to enable her to not issue marriage licenses stands a conservative Christian set of values and statements that have shaped U.S. society, as well as a version of Christian beliefs and histories that have shaped societies over millennia. This historical weight behind claiming God's authority and the inseparability of Davis's beliefs from her being provide a huge bolster to the authority she enacts in this conversation.

Who Can Speak for Love?

Whereas only one of the primary interlocutors, Davis, has the availability to speak on behalf of God, more of the interlocutors speak on behalf of love, including Moore and Ermold as well as many of the gathered crowd of protestors.

```
72   MOORE:   ((looking at his partner)) that's what I'm paying for. I'm paying (.) for this
73            memory (.) with my partner that >I love, that I have been with for seventeen
74            years<. ((flapping on the counter this his right hand)) What's the longest
75            you've been with someone, that you've been married to someone?
```

In line 73, Moore claims his love for his partner as the reason why he is demanding to get a marriage license. Invoking love in his argument, as well as the length of his relationship, connects with a line of arguments made in favor of same-sex marriage.

Those who advocated for same-sex marriage often argued that to deny same-sex marriage also denied a basic human right, or at least a constitutional one (Tracy, 2009; Tracy & Hughes, 2014). The U.S. Constitution provides legal support for freedom of expression and association, which proponents for same-sex marriage argue includes whom one loves and the type of partnerships they should enjoy. Although the U.S. Constitution bolsters this particular web of relations of power, it also connects to arguments made against same-sex marriage through the freedom of religion. Those who agree with Davis would envision that this provision means that marriage should remain a sacred covenant recognized in the Christian definition of one man and one woman.

Later in the interaction, in line 200, Moore points out that "not everyone believes what you believe."

```
200   MOORE:   [Not everyone believes what you believe=
201   DAVIS:   =That's your choice, [that's your choice
202   MOORE:                         [you're creating a religion in this office-
203   DAVIS:   No I'm [not ((shaking her head))
```

This sequence highlights a particular view of the *scene* in which this interaction takes place and a disagreement about whether acting under God's authority means the scene is religious. Moore's argument here relies on the freedom of religion provision in the U.S. Constitution, in that "everyone" should have the freedom to believe what they will and that Davis's creation of "a religion in this office" prohibits that freedom. It is also notable that Moore does not rely on love as an authoritative source here, and love is left out of explicit mention through the rest of this interaction. Instead, he engages on the authoritative grounds of God and religion.

Finally, in line 201, we see the weights of the authorities of God and love come to bear against each other with these participants. Davis, who claimed her beliefs are inseparable from her, affords a different weight to those of Moore and Ermold, whose arguments do not carry the same historical weight of millennia of religious writing, thought, and belief. Davis marks Moore and Ermold's beliefs as a choice. The couple's belief in equal rights, the power of love, or whatever else may be glossed under their "belief" in this interaction is therefore a choice they made. In this way, Davis draws on decades of arguments against LGBTQ people that portray their sexual orientation as choice and thereby separable from them because they could choose otherwise.

The right to choose whom to love and to marry them is a relatively recent societal accomplishment compared to the Christian mandate to carry out God's authority. Through the acts each participant makes in the conversation, we see that those involving God as a co-participant, since he "cannot be separated" from Davis, carry more weight. Love, however, is sparingly used as an explicit co-participant and is eventually left out of explicit mention, whereas Davis continues to speak in religious terms.

Cultural Discourse Theory

Trudy Milburn

This section follows the ethnography of communication by delving into one related methodological offshoot from that tradition known as cultural discourse analysis (CuDA). With CuDA, analysts examine "cultural premises" that are enacted during the interaction between Kim Davis, David Ermold, and David Moore (Carbaugh, 2007; Scollo, 2011). When using this approach, analysts posit cultural premises about communication that participants draw upon and enact when speaking. They become evident to analysts by a close reading and by examining patterned practices in which participants engage.

Carbaugh has described five "hubs and radiants of meaning" that are essentially messages about or conjure senses of being, acting, emoting, relating, and dwelling (Carbaugh, 2007). The terminology of hubs and radiants is based on a wheel metaphor whereby one of the five becomes the central focus, or hub, and the other four radiate out from that hub. An analyst examines discourse for these hub/radiant relationships when attempting to understand specific cultural premises of communication. By focusing on *being*, and examining specific references to persons or objects of interaction, we can address questions about (im)material dimensions of the beings incorporated or brought to life in talk. By further noting the radiants present within an interaction, including information about how people act and relate to one another, participants in the interaction may reveal agonistic cultural premises (Philipsen, 1986; Carbaugh, 1988/1989; Covarrubias & Saito, 2019) that demonstrate how their specific premises may be at odds, fundamentally.

Conflicting Cultural Premises

Within the present interaction, observers immediately notice that Davis's claim that she's acting "under God's authority" (line 49) is stated but not elaborated. What Davis leaves "unsaid" is a response to any of the previous questions asking her to say more. She simply changes the subject (line 55). After stating plainly in line 49, "under God's authority," Davis demonstrates that no further rejoinders about this statement are warranted, and she asks her interlocutors to leave (line 55).

```
47  ERMOLD:   Under [whose authority? (0.5) are you not issuing [licenses?
48  MOORE:          [Why
49  DAVIS:                                        [Under God's authority
50             ((looking defiantly at David Ermold))
51  OTHER:    Did the lawyers tell you-
52  MOORE:    [Did God tell you to do this? Did God tell you how to treat us (.) like this?
53  ERMOLD:   [I don't believe in your god. I don't believe in your god. I don't believe in
54             your [god
55  DAVIS:               [((looking at Moore)) I've asked you all to leave, you are interrupting
56             [my business ((opening her arms))
```

Several CuDA studies allude to the way silence is used for what has been referred to as "(un)sayables" by some American Indians (Covarrubias & Windchief, 2009; Basso, 1996; Carbaugh, Berry, & Numikari-Berry, 2006; Carbaugh, 1999; Milstein, 2008; Molina-Markham, 2012; Scollo, 2004). As these studies illustrate, "the cultural boundaries of what can and ought to be communicated, to whom, and with what consequences are explored" (Van Over, Dori-Hacohen, & Winchatz, 2019). However, within any particular interaction we can find that supposedly "inexpressible claims" are "sayable with little trouble," and yet often we find that, "speakers often do offer accounts for their wordlessness as part of the conversational turn in which they claim that something cannot be said, potentially to remediate issues of perceived incompetence" (van Over, n.d., p. 7).

In this particular interaction, Davis's invocation of God and her subsequent silence on this topic is contrasted by Moore's repeated questions, including, "Did God tell you to do this?" (line 52). Moore's statements seem to indicate an alternate set of cultural assumptions that material actions prompted by a reference to "God" are unacceptable to him and require further elaboration rather than silence. The additional assertions made by the others in the scene, "God doesn't run the government" (lines 132–133) and "this is not a house of God" (line 135), align with Moore's request for elaboration and put God as the subject who can do things (*take action*) in certain material places (*dwellings*).

```
128  MCKINNEY:            [We're praying for God and God's word and
129             find solace= ((raising his right hand toward the ceiling))
130  ERMOLD:   =God (.) [does not belong in the county clerk's office ((bending toward Kim
131             Davis as she is getting back to them))
132  OTHER:        [God doesn't run the government!
133  OTHER:    God doesn't run the government!
134             ((Kim Davis is back in front of Ermold and Moore))
135  OTHER:    This is not a house of God!
```

Both sets of cultural assumptions are well grounded in the hub of *being* which indicates the way personhood (or those given the status of persons) is expressed and enacted. This is succinctly expressed by Davis when she says, "No my beliefs cannot be separated from me" (line 184). In this articulation, we hear beliefs materialized in *being*. The actions one takes within this particular set of assumptions about being indicate future consequences. Davis notes, "I'm willing to face my consequences" (line 195) that stem from individual "choices" (line 201).

```
193   DAVIS:                                      [I'm not saying your lives are
194              not worth- I hm- You are putting words in my mouth and that will not do. I
195              simply told you all, I'm willing to face my consequences and you will all face
196              your consequences when it comes time for judgment=
197   MOORE:     =We don't have conse[quences I don't believe in your judgment
198   DAVIS:                          [It's plain and simple
199   PARTNER 2: Not everyone believes [the way you believe
200   MOORE:                              [Not everyone believes what you believe=
201   DAVIS:     =That's your choice, [that's your choice
202   MOORE:                          [you're creating a religion in this office-
203   DAVIS:     No I'm [not ((shaking her head))
204   PARTNER 2:        [Yes you are
```

Moore's cultural premise can be stated as "people have rights to their beliefs but should not take away others' rights (to their own beliefs)." Moore creates an agonistic set of premises when he articulates, "we don't have consequences, I don't believe in your judgment" (line 197). *Being* for Moore is not grounded in the same set of beliefs as Davis. Moore separates his beliefs into categories, those belonging to the realm of "religion" and those that are grounded in "love."

Interestingly, Moore also includes an unsayable when he asserts that he loves his partner (line 73).

```
72   MOORE   ((looking at his partner)) that's what I'm paying for. I'm paying (.) for this
73           memory (.) with my partner that >I love, that I have been with for seventeen
74           years<. ((flapping on the counter this his right hand)) What's the longest
75           you've been with someone, that you've been married to someone?
```

An American cultural premise that suggests that emotions are often difficult to articulate is foregrounded here (see also Carbaugh, 1995). In this set of premises, it can "go without saying" that two people who are together for seventeen years are in love; however, by stating "that I love" (line 73), Moore takes the statement out of the unsayable category and makes an assertion about *relating*. The relationship between Moore and his long-time partner is encoded into *being*.

For Davis and her supporters, the radiant of *relating* is also used. For instance, we hear the old clerk stating "we're praying for God and God's word and find solace" (lines 128–9). This statement indicates that the relationship between God and those who believe in him materializes him as a being with which others can have a relationship.

CuDA is one set of tools that can be used to illustrate the way that God and love are materialized into *being* within a particular interaction. Further, by focusing on the discursive hub of being specifically, we can explore the ways beings *act* and *relate* to one another and how participants create agonistic tensions based on opposing cultural premises they use or call upon to make their claims. By using CuDA to examine each set of cultural premises, we learn more about how those who so speak are able to materialize their key premises as the source of their authority in the conversation.

Love vs. God: Two Symmetrical Authorities in Theory, One Winner in Practice?

Bertrand Fauré

Knowing if something or someone is more or less material in a given situation is crucial to understand where authority comes from and how it works in practice. Ultimately, authority is material when important things cannot be done without its presence (Taylor & Van Every, 2014). Kim Davis's refusal matters because it is important for David Ermold and David Moore to be married. Absence matters. How to know if something is rendered more or less (im)material during interaction? In order to answer this question, this chapter focuses on two apparently very abstract authoritative figures (God and Love[1]) and crosses various methods for analyzing their materialization during the interaction. While the three previous analyses suggest that God is effectively the highest source of authority for Kim Davis but that Love is just one authority among others materialized by David Ermold and David Moore during the interaction, this section puts forward three reasons why Love should be seen as the symmetrical highest source of authority opposed by the couple to the one of Davis's God.

First, God and Love are the first sources of authority respectively claimed by each party early on in this interaction. It is clear with Kim Davis when she refuses to deliver the marriage license "Under God's Authority" (line 49) that she places God above everything else (the Supreme Court, her job, public opinion, etc.) on her personal authority scale. Before being on the good side of the law and of the camera, Ermold and Moore also have defied, to some extent, their country's laws and norms and taken the risk to lose their jobs. Similarly to Davis, they place something above everything else on their personal authority scale, something that has given them the force to come out despite public blame, something constructed in time and that cannot be denied by

Davis, namely Love. This primacy is clear when they ask, "How many times have you been married?" (line 21), knowing that she has been married four times in contradiction to her God's law and thus suggesting that she also places Love above God. Given that Ermold and Moore have been together for seventeen years ("the partner that I love and I've been with for seventeen years," lines 73–74), this, in their reasoning, ultimately places the authority of their Love above that of Davis's God.

Second, the struggle between God and Love as sources of authority is not only central in this interaction but also in the broader narrative in which this interaction is embedded. It is not for nothing that the recent book about Kim Davis is entitled *Under God's Authority: The Kim Davis Story* (Davis, Aman, & Staver, 2018): it is what gives her force and support from her community from the beginning of the affair. On the other hand, the couple's fight is a particular case of a broader "Love wins" revendication. Their interaction in 2016 was not a minor issue but was rather reflective of the political division between conservatives and liberals in the United States. Of course, equal rights and freedom are globally progressing, but bigotry and discrimination still resist, often in the name of Love (of the country, of God, of the community).

The same applies during the interaction. All of this happens because Ermold and Moore had visited Davis's office several times. What is materialized first by this reiterated presence is their continuing, emotional relation. If Davis had agreed to provide the marriage license initially, the subsequent confrontation would not have occurred. If Ermold and Moore had not cared, they would not have come back again and again. What also gives weight and materiality to the interaction examined herein is Davis's reiterated refusal to issue them their marriage license (i.e., the absence of legal authorization). This exchange is particularly salient because the legal context had recently changed, turning upside down the position of each party. At the moment, Davis knows that the battle is lost and that the two men in front of her will have no mercy if she keeps resisting. Indeed, they could go elsewhere. If they are here, covered by the press, it is also in order to force her to do what she has always refused to do.

All this hate accumulated against Davis is strongly materialized by Ermold and Moore during the interaction in contradiction with their claim of being led by Love and in sharp contrast with Davis's calm, politeness, and self-control. Both parties indeed are reaching the limits of this dead-end dialogue. They know that this demand and this refusal are the last one and that the next step will be the court. Nobody can know at this time that the fight would be still going on for several years and that this interaction will be part of a legend. However, the video recording of this interaction became viral because many elements making such a future possible were present. By a spectacular reversal of the situation, the former heroes of Love became the hangmen of their previous hang-woman, who became a hero of God for her resistance and sacrifice.

Third, focusing on these two sources of authority enables us to study in detail how such seemingly abstract entities can become materialized during interaction. Further, we explore the part played by this material-ization in the performing/enactment of authority. How to make authority material is an old philosophical question that remains vivid across the social sciences. How do interlocutors know which source of authority is the highest and when? Can we speak in terms of degree of materiality/materialization? What can we learn about the materialization of author-ity from the fierce exchanges between Davis, Ermold, and Moore?

Organizational members, and especially public servants such as Davis, are not supposed to place God or Love above the law and other bureau-cratic rules. The interaction taking place in the Rowan County office illustrates what sometimes happens when a single authority system is not agreed upon, as when religious beliefs and sexual orientation come onto the stage: moral outrage on each part, and attempts to restore hierarchy between principles, rules, and values, lead to what appears to the other party as insanity, rage, and, in some cases, bad business. On the other hand, this situation may also illustrate how people find the force to make change possible—or resist to it—even against strong odds. Whether we agree or not with Kim Davis's convictions, we cannot deny her courage and self-control in this situation.

This woman would never turn into a bureaucratic Eichmann, applying mechanically the inhuman order of a human authority (Arendt, 1994). Her humanity here comes from her capacity to resist and disobey human order by placing herself under a higher non-human authority (God). As Ermold and Moore know too well, Davis can also be a merciless execu-tor of human orders when these orders fit with what she perceived as God's law. But she became a hero by incarnating resistance to human authority in the name of something greater, not obedience. On the other hand, Ermold and Moore were heroic when fighting together against dis-crimination and now incarnate the defense of the new law. Organizations should pay more attention to such situations that might well be excep-tional (i.e., as exemplary rather than mistake) but may greatly influence the work that may be conducted going forward.

Discussion

Thus far, we have considered the question about (im)materiality from the vantage of four lenses. In the first, we adopted a constitutive view of communication to show that God and love acquire various degrees of materiality (and authority) during this interaction in the sense that the interactants position them as passing through (or translating in) a greater or smaller number of beings and actions. The second analysis illustrated the way the ethnography of communication, as expressed by Hymes (1973, 1974), could be used to focus on the societal weight behind the (im)material sources of authority in the courthouse interaction. The third analysis used cultural discourse analysis expressed by Carbaugh to draw connections between what may have been unsayable and immaterial into sayable and material being. In the fourth, we considered the twin pillars of God and Love in a verbal duel whereby each interlocutor places one into the highest position of authority. In all of these analyses we recognize the way authority begins to materialize as God or Love when what was immaterial (or unsayable) becomes sayable in a particular interactional moment.

Although we have brought different literatures to bear when examining this scene, we all concur that this exercise helps to demonstrate the utility of a constitutional approach to interaction. We have approached the question about how to consider the materiality of authority of God and love from *within* the interaction at the courthouse in 2016. In addition, we placed that interaction in a larger context by considering *external* material conditions as reasons interactants place God and love as the most prominent material beings.

The presentation of our joint analyses was intended to illustrate distinct approaches to questions about authority and power. We believe the distinct lenses provide possible alternatives to viewing God and love as different objects that become material and how they might be used towards particular ends within an interaction. If the cultural premises of the participants do not align, then a hierarchy cannot be set up to create a winner of an argument. The trick, in this case, was for interlocutors to use the materialization of God and love to make the more persuasive claim; not only for purposes of a debate but also for the enactment of real material differences—the granting of a marriage license. For David Ermold and David Moore, they believed that love would win the day because of a premise that only those "in love" would marry and remain married (Kim Davis's multiple marriages demonstrate lack of "true love"); conversely, Kim Davis's assertion that God's authority determined her actions to forbid granting the license indicates her strongly held belief that there is no higher authority than God.

The other conclusion is the importance of this study for organizational scholars. The relevant state authority, in this case a courthouse where a marriage license is issued, is an organizational workplace. As such, the setting is an important place where things are materialized into being for a variety of purposes. By focusing on the atypical beings materialized in this scenario—God and love—and their actions and relations to the other participants, organizational scholars may begin to anticipate future scenarios whereby otherwise immaterial entities may be brought into being for quite different purposes.

Table 5.1 Summary of Analytical Approaches to (Im)Material Authority

Perspective	The Constitutive view of communication Thomas Martine	Ethnography of communication Katherine Peters	Cultural discourse analysis Trudy Milburn	Symmetrical authorities Bertrand Fauré
Analytical focus	How beings materialize (i.e., acquire their properties) by relating to other beings during a conversation	How speech events serve as a locus for language to interact with life and produce cultural forms	How cultural premises are displayed or able to be located within discursive practices	Understanding which authority between Davis's God vs. the couple's Love is more or less materialized and makes the difference at the end
How authority is constituted in interaction	Something acquires authority by expressing itself through other beings, thereby presenting itself as what connects or unifies these beings.	Through speech acts in sequence used by particular participants toward different ends, and ultimately with differing results	By saying the formerly unsayable to muster authority	The authority of Davis and her God is constituted by rendering absent something that matters for the couple.
How it shifts understanding of authority	Authority is closely related to the process of materializing (which is also the process by which something persists in being).	Authority is enacted within the interaction, which relies on cultural and historical understandings of language-in-society.	Authority is brought into *being* and can alter how people *act* and *relate*.	Authority is negotiated through such situations where its absence matters.
Key concepts	Relational ontology, being-as-other, materializing in others	SPEAKING framework, speech event, speech act	Hubs/radiants of being, acting, relating, dwelling, emoting	Authority, absence
Suggested readings	Latour (2013), Benoit-Barné and Cooren (2009), and Cooren (2015)	Blommaert (2009) and Hymes (1973, 1974)	Carbaugh (2007), Scollo (2011) and Scollo and Milburn (2019)	Taylor, J. R. & Van Every, E. J. (2014). *When organization fails: Why authority matters*. New York, NY: Routledge.

Note

1. In this section, we capitalize the word Love to stress the parity between God and Love.

References

Aakhus, M., Ballard, D., Flanagin, A. J., Kuhn, T., Leonardi, P., Mease, J., & Miller, K. (2011). Communication and materiality: A conversation from the CM cafe´. *Communication Monographs*, 78(4), 557–568. https://doi.org/10.10 80/03637751.2011.618358

Arendt, H. (1994). *Eichmann in Jerusalem*. New York, NY: Penguin Books.

Barad, K. (2007). *Meeting the universe halfway: Quantum physics and the entanglement of matter and meaning*. Durham, NC: Duke University Press.

Basso, K. (1996). *Wisdom sits in places: Landscape and language among the Western Apache*. Albuquerque, NM: University of New Mexico Press.

Benoit-Barné, C., & Cooren, F. (2009). The accomplishment of authority through presentification: How authority is distributed among and negotiated by organizational members. *Management Communication Quarterly*, 23(1), 5–31. https://doi.org/10.1177/0893318909335414

Blommaert, J. (2009). Ethnography and democracy: Hymes's political theory of language. *Text & Talk*, 29(3), 257–276. https://doi.org/10.1515/TEXT. 2009.014

Carbaugh, D. (1988/1989). Deep agony: "Self" vs. "society" in Donahue discourse. *Research on Language and Social Interaction*, 22, 179–212. https://doi.org/ 10.1080/08351818809389302

Carbaugh, D. (1995). "Are Americans really superficial?": Notes on Finnish and American cultures in linguistic action. In L. Salo-Lee (Ed.), *Kieli & julttuuri* (pp. 269–297). Jyvaskyla, Finland: Publications of the Department of Communication, University of Jyvaskyla.

Carbaugh, D. (1999). "Just listen": "Listening" and landscape among the Blackfeet. *Western Journal of Communication*, 63(3), 250–270. https://doi.org/10.1080/ 10570319909374641

Carbaugh, D. (2007). Cultural discourse analysis: Communication practices and intercultural encounters. *Journal of Intercultural Communication Research*, 36(3), 167–182. https://doi.org/10.1080/17475750701737090

Carbaugh, D., Berry, M., & Numikari-Berry, M. (2006). Coding personhood through cultural terms and practices: Silence and quietude as a Finnish "natural way of being". *Journal of Language and Social Psychology*, 25, 203–220. https://doi.org/10.1177/0261927X06289422

Cooren, F. (2012). Communication theory at the center: Ventriloquism and communicative construction of reality. *Journal of Communication*, 62, 1–20. https:// doi.org/10.1111/j.1460-2466.2011.01622.x

Cooren, F. (2015). *In medias res*: Communication, existence, and materiality. *Communication Research and Practice*, 1(4), 307–321. https://doi.org/10.108 0/22041451.2015.1110075

Cooren, F., & Sandler, S. (2014). Polyphony, ventriloquism, and constitution: In dialogue with Bakhtin. *Communication Theory*, 24(3), 225–244. https://doi. org/10.1111/comt.12041

Covarrubias, K., & Saito, M. (2019). Symbolic agonistics: Stressing emotion and relation in Mexican, Mexican@, and Japanese discourses. In M. Scollo & T. Milburn (Eds.), *Engaging and transforming global communication through cultural discourse analysis: A tribute to Donal Carbaugh*. Madison, NJ: Farleigh Dickinson Press.

Covarrubias, P. O., & Windchief, S. R. (2009). Silences in stewardship: Some American Indian college student examples. *The Howard Journal of Communication, 20*(4), 333–352. https://doi.org/10.1080/10646170903300754

Davis, K., Aman, J., & Staver, M. (2018). *Under God's authority: The Kim Davis story*. Maitland, FL: Liberty Counsel.

Fiske, J. (1990). Review of talking American: Cultural discourses on Donahue by D. Carbaugh. *Quarterly Journal of Speech, 76*, 450–451. https://doi.org/10.1080/00335639009383936

Fiske, J. (1991). Writing ethnographies: Contribution to a dialogue. *Quarterly Journal of Speech, 77*, 330–335. https://doi.org/10.1080/00335639109383964

Hoopes, J. (Ed.). (1991). *Peirce on signs: Writing on semiotic*. Chapel Hill, NC: University of North Carolina Press.

Hymes, D. (1973). Speech and language: On the origins and foundations of inequality among speakers. *Daedalus, 102*(3), 59–85.

Hymes, D. (1974). *Foundations in sociolinguistics: An ethnographic approach*. Philadelphia, PA: University of Pennsylvania Press.

Latour, B. (2013). *An inquiry into modes of existence: An anthropology of the moderns*. Cambridge, MA: Harvard University Press.

Martine, T., & Cooren, F. (2016). A relational approach to materiality and organizing: The case of a creative idea. In *Beyond interpretivism? New encounters with technology and organization* (p. 143–166). Cham: Springer. https://doi.org/10.1007/978-3-319-49733-4_9

Martine, T., Cooren, F., & Bartels, G. (2017). Evaluating creativity through the degrees of solidity of its assessment: A relational approach. *The Journal of Creative Behavior*. https://doi.org/10.1002/jocb.219

Milstein, T. (2008). When whales "speak for themselves": Communication as a mediating force in wildlife tourism. *Environmental Communication, 2*(2), 173–192. https://doi.org/10.1080/17524030802141745

Molina-Markham, E. (2012). Lives that preach: The cultural dimensions of telling one's "spiritual journey" among Quakers. *Narrative Inquiry, 22*(1), 3–23. https://doi.org/10.1075/ni.22.1.02mol

Philipsen, G. (1986). Mayor Daley's council speech: A cultural analysis. *Quarterly Journal of Speech, 72*, 247–260. https://doi.org/10.1080/00335638609383772

Putnam, L., & Nicotera, A. M. (Ed.). (2009). *Building theories of organization: The constitutive role of communication*. New York, NY: Routledge.

Scollo, C., & Milburn, T. (Eds.). (2019). *Engaging and transforming global communication through cultural discourse analysis: A tribute to Donal Carbaugh*. Madison, NJ: Farleigh Dickinson Press.

Scollo, M. (2004). Nonverbal ways of communicating with nature: A cross-case study. In S. L. Senecah (Ed.), *The environmental communication yearbook* (pp. 227–249). Mahwah, NJ: Lawrence Erlbaum.

Scollo, M. (2011). Cultural approaches to discourse analysis: A theoretical and methodological conversation with special focus on Donal Carbaugh's cultural discourse theory. *Journal of Multicultural Discourses*, 6(1), 1–32. https://doi.org/10.1080/17447143.2010.536550

Taylor, J. R., & Cooren, F. (1997). What makes communication "organizational"? How the many voices of a collectivity become the one voice of an organization. *Journal of Pragmatics*, 27, 409–438. https://doi.org/10.1016/S0378-2166 (96)00044-6

Taylor, J. R., & Van Every, E. (2014). *When organization fails: Why authority matters*. New York, NY: Routledge.

Tracy, K. (2009). How questioning constructs judge identities: Oral argument about same-sex marriage. *Discourse Studies*, 11(2), 199–221. https://doi.org/10.1177/1461445608100944

Tracy, K., & Hughes, J. M. F. (2014). Democracy-appealing partisanship: A situated ideal of citizenship. *Journal of Applied Communication Research*, 42(3), 307–324. doi: 10.1080/00909882.2014.911940

van Over, B. (n.d.). *The cultural boundaries of the sayable: Three codes for the use and interpretation of claims of the inexpressible*. Unpublished conference paper.

van Over, B., Dori-Hacohen, G., & Winchatz, M. (2019). Policing the boundaries of the sayable: The public negotiation of profane, prohibited and proscribed speech. In M. Scollo & T. Milburn (Eds.), *Engaging and transforming global communication through cultural discourse analysis: A tribute to Donal Carbaugh*. Madison, NJ: Farleigh Dickinson Press.

6   Decentering the Analysis

The Authority of Spectators, Journalists and Others

Chantal Benoit-Barné, Sky Marsen, Nan Wang, and Yue Yang

Authority is often understood as taking place between two parties, typically an authority holder—for instance an organizational superior—and a person with less authority—a subordinate. In this interaction, such a conventional framing draws attention to the exchange between Davis and the couple. However, the analysis could be decentered to include a broader range of people and objects into the equation, including those who do not speak. In this chapter, we present four different approaches to the construction of authority and power. However, contrary to other contributions in this book, we relate to a broader range of participants than those involved in the central interaction between Kim Davis, David Moore and David Ermold.

Despite theoretical and methodological differences among the four approaches, we all aim to answer some key questions:

1. What are some ways to analyze authority (and, by extension for some of us, power) in interactions that appear marginal at first sight?
2. How can we account for decision-making and meaning-making as distinct processes in the establishment of authority?
3. What are the contexts in which authority is constructed and negotiated?

We agree that what is "marginal" or "decentered" depends on how we define the center. We also agree that decision-making and meaning-making take place through the manipulation of signs in language and talk in interaction. For all of us, authority is constructed and negotiated through discourse, which includes both the talk of the participants and the multimodal signs (both visual and verbal) of the way this talk is performed and presented.

Chantal Benoit-Barné begins the discussion with an overview of a perspective on authority as an effect of presence and the accomplishment of authority as a relational negotiation (see also Benoit-Barné & Cooren, 2009). This approach emphasizes the relations that are created throughout the sequence as actors associate and dissociate from each other and from a host of entities, thus shaping the situation in which they find themselves. Second, Sky Marsen focuses on the narrator's role in performing authority through organizing how the text is presented. Her approach is informed by narrative-semiotic theory and builds on the premise that, by presenting this interaction to the viewer, the narrator-presenter assumes meaning-making ability and, by extension, authority, without playing a role in the interaction itself.

Then, Yue Yang analyzes media-power-in-interaction in three encounters between the applicants and Kim Davis. She finds that the meaningful construction and negotiation over relationships and identities in situations influence interactants' orientation to media as something agentic or powerful. Finally, Nan Wang uses a conversation analysis approach, focusing on the interactional process between David Moore and the journalists and other couples. The analysis showcases how power and authority are constructed and oriented to between these social actors on a moment-by-moment and turn-by-turn basis.

The chapter is organized with each writer presenting her approach and providing answers to the key questions described above. It ends with a short synthesis of salient points.

A Relational View of Authority

Chantal Benoit-Barné

In order to account for the spectators, journalists and office workers' roles in the accomplishment of authority, we first need to move away from a static view of authority, narrowly conceived as the property of individuals (individuals *are* authorities by virtue of expertise, office, abilities to talk and govern, etc.) or structures (authority resides in hierarchies, procedures, norms, etc.), to account for the dynamic process whereby authority can be established and negotiated in interaction by all those involved. This move also entails broadening our understanding of 1) what counts as an expression of authority and 2) the many implications authority may have for collective action as a whole.

We tend to link authority to decision-making whether by asking who has the most influence on the decision-making process or who ultimately decides—in this case, who decides whether a license will be issued or not (see Benoit-Barné & Fox, 2017 for a discussion of this trend). Although decision-making authority and the ability to shape the decision-making process are certainly important to consider when investigating the dynamics of authority in this sequence, they do not, from the standpoint of the analytical perspective presented here, provide a full picture of the phenomenon. The authority to shape the meaning of a situation and its overall influence for the larger controversy over same-sex marriage, a controversy unfolding at this particular moment in time via this particular interaction but in no way limited to it, are also important to consider.

I propose adopting a relational view of authority that can account for the many different ways in which authority can be established and negotiated by all those involved in an interaction with varying degrees of influence. In keeping with a communication-as-constitutive perspective (CCO), I advance a view of authority as essentially communicational and relational (see in particular Benoit-Barné & Cooren, 2009; Taylor & Van Every, 2014; Benoit-Barné & Fox, 2017). From this perspective, authority is a property of relationships communicatively generated and negotiated in the process of organizing. Authority, thus, is not a static property of either individuals (in the form of charisma or expertise, for instance) or organizational structures (such as hierarchy or chain of command). Rather, it emerges and is negotiated through an ongoing communicative process of coorientation as those involved in an interaction relate to each other and to objects of interest to them. As such, authority is conceived as both emergent and dynamic, created and sustained through interactions and communication.

It is important to emphasize that this theoretical positioning toward authority as an emergent and dynamic propriety of relations (re)established through interaction does not imply that authority is evanescent. Authority is a legitimate form of power linked to order and stability because its local emergence and negotiation involve a process of "presentification" whereby established and recognizable entities are brought to bear on the interaction. The notion of presentification is informed by Gumbrecht (2004) and Cooren (2006; Cooren, Brummans, & Charrieras, 2008). It refers to ways of speaking and acting by which actors can make present things and beings that influence the unfolding of the situation in which they find themselves.

These entities can consist of texts, material objects, ideals, norms, hierarchies, etc. They may be physically absent from or present in the interaction, although occupying a seemingly peripheral place. In both cases, the act of presentification is placing them at the foreground, linking them to what is currently happening. For instance, we can see how Davis relies on the Sixth Circuit and on God to support her position, while Moore evokes love and, later on, the neutrality of government to make his point. Both presentify a number of entities to give weight to their stance and influence the unfolding of the interaction. From the standpoint of a relational view of authority, it is both the actors and the entities they presentify (their association) that are conceived as contributing to the accomplishment of authority.

On the basis of these ideas, the main research question that arises is not who has *the* authority in the interaction under study, but rather how authority is established and negotiated by all those involved in the interaction and how this process (that Taylor & Van Every, 2014 refer to as a process of authoring) influences the unfolding of the interaction. In other words, this perspective implies that the journalists, the spectators and the office workers play a role in how authority emerges and is negotiated throughout the sequence as they are in relation with each other and with Davis and the couple. It does not mean that they necessarily have the same role and carry the same weight as Davis or the two couples asking for a marriage license, which is an issue that needs to be settled empirically. Rather, it means that they must be theoretically conceived and empirically studied as equally significant for our understanding of how authority emerges and shapes social interactions because they are part of the web of relations that constitutes authority in this particular interaction.

More specifically, adopting this perspective to study the interaction entails that we pay attention to the relations that are created and sustained as actors interact with each other; these actors associate and dissociate from each other and from a host of entities, thus shaping the situation in which they all find themselves. This analysis emphasizes the following three key issues and processes:

Backing the Main Actors (Davis, Moore and Ermold) by Voicing Ideas in Keeping With Their Respective Position

Throughout the sequence, we can hear individuals who make statements that support the opinions expressed by either Moore or Davis. Consider, for instance, the words of McKinney, who evokes God and the words of God on line 128. This is a form of support that contributes to Davis's authority because it occurs in the background in a way that does not divert from her actions yet gives them more weight. The same process occurs with Moore as spectators shout, "Do your job! Do your job! Do your job" (line 96), in support of his claim that, contrary to what Davis is asking, he will not leave the office or back away from the counter. These manifestations of support reflect the relational nature of authority. They allow us to see that both Davis's and Moore's authority rest on the presence and words of actors other than themselves. Davis establishes her authority in association with the clerk (and many other actors and entities that have not yet been discussed). The same can be said of Moore, whose authority relies on the presence and words of his own allies. These actors should in fact be conceived as co-authors involved in a process of co-authoring Davis's and Moore's authority in this sequence.

The Creation of Collective Actors and How It Contributes to the Establishment and Negotiation of Authority

This point relates to how both Davis and Moore address a group rather than individuals on several occasions during the interaction. Kim Davis addresses the crowd in front of her, creating a collective actor distinct from the individuals that she directly speaks to and engages with during the sequence, namely Moore, Ermold, partner 1 and partner 2. She uses the expression "you all" seven times, for instance, in line 23, "I just want you all to know that we are not issuing marriage licenses today," or in lines 55–62, "I've asked you all to leave, you are interrupting my business." By addressing the group of people facing her rather than Moore or Ermold who are questioning her directly, she is in fact eluding their questions and showing that she does not have to/want to engage with them as individuals. She is asserting her authority as head of this office while also recognizing that the large crowd occupying her office is part of the problem she is faced with, thus broadening the stakes of the interaction.

This process also characterizes the dynamics from the point of view of Moore's intervention. Moore addresses Davis and the office employees as a group in lines 104–108, "YOU SHOULD BE ASHAMED OF YOURSELF! EVERYONE IN THIS OFFICE SHOULD be ashamed of themselves," and again in lines 120–122, "YOUR CHILDREN WILL HAVE TO LOOK AT YOU AND REALIZE THAT YOU ARE BIGOTS." In doing so, Moore addresses the office employees as full-fledged actors (and as bigots), thus also broadening the stakes of the interaction as the office workers become Davis's de facto silent allies. Overall, we can see that this process of creating and addressing collective actors is essential to understanding how actors who may appear *in peripheria*, such as clerks and journalists in this sequence, do in fact become essential to the negotiation of authority.

Dissociating From a Collective Actor and Thereby Contributing to the Establishment and Negotiation of Authority

In line with the previous point, it is also noteworthy how the participants dissociate themselves from collective actors. The sequence from lines 163 to 173 is particularly interesting in that regard. By telling reporters to "shut up" and then inviting two people from the crowd to come to the front and speak directly to Davis, Moore creates a new distinction: the crowd is not, as Davis suggested, a united collective actor; reporters are their own entity distinct from those who are there to apply for a marriage license. This dissociation is interesting because it goes against Davis's framing of the situation as one in which journalists and activists are allied. If they are not allied, are they distinct actors and what is in fact the nature of their connection? The fact that the potential players are multiplying and that the relations between them are ambiguous makes the situation all the more difficult for Davis to manage.

All in all, these three points illustrate what it means to say that authority is relational. We can see that actors must rely on each other to establish and negotiate their authority in interaction. They associate and dissociate from both collective and individual actors. They also rely on several entities that they presentify through their actions and speech (God, love, the Sixth Circuit Court, etc.). None of the actors are in fact acting and establishing their authority alone. As such, the journalists, the spectators and the office workers are important to consider because they are part of the web of relations that constitutes authority in this interaction.

The Narrator's Role in Constructing Authority

Sky Marsen

When we watch this video we are, in effect, watching and interpreting the episode of a story. We distinguish individual characters (and may even recognize a few from other stories, as often happens in films with celebrities, which is what these characters actually are); attribute motivations to them through their actions and words; identify with some and distance ourselves from others; and notice causal connections between events. Following this line of reasoning, this chapter uses a narrative-semiotic approach and discusses the narrator's role in the presentation of events (Herman, 2009; Marsen, 2006).

There are many ways to approach narrative. Although narrative is sometimes equated with story (a representation of events with a beginning, middle and end), story is actually only one component of the genre. Narratologists generally distinguish two (Chatman, 1978; Prince, 2003) or three (Genette, 1983; Bal, 1993) levels of narrative. Adopting the dual division, we have the level of the story (the events, actions and agents) and the level of discourse (the way in which the story is presented—including the temporal ordering, duration and frequency of actions, points of view, and speakers). All these techniques together create the device of the "narrator," the source whose discourse "filters" and organizes the story.

"Authority" shares etymological roots with "author," and, as we know since the era of structuralism in the 1970s, the author is dead (Barthes, 1977). In other words, the creator of a text is not the only one responsible for the meanings attributed to the text by readers or viewers, the same way that authority is not intentional but contextual and circumstantial—one cannot impose authority on a situation without the necessary social conditions according to which authority is measured and conferred. For example, as has been aptly illustrated by speech act theory, I cannot sentence a person to a prison sentence just by uttering the words unless I am a judge and the setting is a courtroom. However, although the author may be dead, the narrator is alive and well. The presence of the text logically implies the presence of a narrator who "manages the exposition, who decides what is to be told, how it is to be told (especially from what point of view, and in what sequence), and what is to be left out" (Jahn, 2001, p. 670). Therefore, the ultimate "authority" for a story lies with the narrator. In filmic narratives, unless there is a voice-over narration, the camera is generally accepted as the narrator.

A focus on the narrator reveals some significant aspects of the video considered here. The story (the text we see) is narrated either from a slightly elevated position (which hides its exact position) or is pivoted on the side of David Moore and the journalists, looking over the desk that separates the two opposing sets of characters. It is, therefore, clearly "on Moore's side," both literally and metaphorically. This position tends to objectify Kim Davis and her employees, as she is consistently the seen object, and subjectifies Moore and the journalists, who are the ones who see. This narratorial technique alone is sufficient to foreground Moore and the journalists and, thereby, to indirectly confer more authority to them than to Davis—the viewer is encouraged to observe what happens from their point of view.

A few other techniques accentuate this. One, there is a constant background sound of clicking of cameras taking photographs, which emphasizes the media presence—it is one of their signifiers—and bolsters their authority. Two, a television screen is continually seen in the office and acts as a background to the action. It constitutes a self-reflexive sign (what structuralist theorists call a *mise en abyme*) signifying the power and ubiquity of the media by mirroring the code (video recording) that produced the text we are seeing. Therefore, these narratorial techniques confer authority to the journalists, who, despite not speaking, are orchestrators of the action. The episode we see is, in many respects, a media text (remembering also that it is found on the *USA Today* website, which "signs off" its media authorship, so to speak).

An internet search revealed no video where Davis or her employees are the narrators of this set of events. This episode in the "Gay Marriage Licensing" story is never presented by Davis or from her point of view. There is, however, at least one other video of the same episode on Moore's YouTube channel (www.youtube.com/watch?v=T7HNVEQ4OmU). This fact increases the frequency in which the story is told—repetition being a framing and foregrounding device that reinforces narratorial authority. In the video on Moore's channel, there is also additional footage that shows Moore leading the camera (the narrator) in the office, thereby marking the relationship between the two. Also, in this version of the story, the camera is very clearly positioned on the citizens' side of the desk, making the narratorial connection with Moore explicit. Therefore, although Davis has governmental (extra-textual) authority, Moore and the journalists have narratorial (textual) authority, which they use to present the situation from a particular perspective, this way implicitly challenging and questioning Davis's state-conferred power to grant licenses.

Another way that the narrator can exert authority on how we perceive an event is by the positioning of agents. Using the actantial model of narrative semiotics (Greimas, 1987), we identify six "actants," which can include both human and non-human agents: Subject (the main agent), Object (the main goal), Sender (the one who asks the Subject to do something, or the motivating factor in wanting to attain the goal), Receiver (the one who receives the Sender's request and is acted upon by it), Helpers and Opponents (the agents that help and oppose the Subject in attaining the goal). The narrator has the power to position a character as the actantial Subject (the protagonist), which also affects who is placed in the Helper and Opponent positions. This way, the narrator attains the power to not only present but also evaluate the recounted events and attempt to influence the audience.

In the video, Moore fills the actantial Subject position, i.e., he is the main character who orients the action. He is not only physically positioned in the space of the narrator, whom he led there, but he also has the most speaking time, initiates the conversation and even acts out the narratorial role of directing others to speak or remain silent. For instance, he tells another agent to be quiet when he thinks this agent is a member of the press and then invites him to come forward and speak when he realizes he is a fellow license seeker, therefore filling the Receiver position together with the other gay license seekers. In addition, his Object is to obtain a marriage license *from Kim Davis* and not from another office. So, Davis is positioned as the Opponent, but, more than this, overcoming her authority becomes an intrinsic part of the Object. Moore does not just want to marry his partner, but, equally it seems, he wants to challenge Davis and her authority. In this he is helped by the Supreme Court ruling that legalized same-sex marriage, as well as by the journalists, who help him tell his story.

Using narrative theory, this section briefly sketched a method to analyze textual constructions of authority and power that focuses on narratorial techniques of presentation. This method examines the role of the narrator and the positioning of agents as ways to claim, challenge and communicate authority, and it moves emphasis away from spoken words or the civic status of participants.

Media-Power-in-Interaction

Yue Yang

When developing a theory that connects power, authority, agency and interpretation, Reed (2017) argues that power should be understood "not simply as logistical capacity but a capacity subject to, and dependent upon, struggles over interpretation" (p. 97). He also stresses that "within a delimited field of vision and division, constituted by an *illusio*, power and authority are very close to the same thing" (Breiger, 2000; Reed, 2017, p. 88). In this analysis, I follow Reed's insights to look at the part played by the media in the interaction and take power as a conceptual extension of authority closely related to interpretation rather than stress their distinction and efface from view "the intermingling of legitimation, interest and coercion" (Reed, 2017, p. 91).

The power of media has attracted much discussion since the beginning of the new century, as our society becomes increasingly media saturated, mediated (Livingstone, 2009) and mediatized (Couldry & Hepp, 2013).

Couldry (2001, 2002) understood media power as the massive concentration of symbolic power—the power of constructing reality (Bourdieu, 1991, p. 166)—in media institutions. In the digital age, where social media and independent channels are also participating in symbolic production and diffusion, Cammaerts, Mattoni, and McCurdy (2013) and other researchers of social movements continue to highlight media power, relating it to the "management of visibility" and the "struggle for recognition" (Thompson, 1995, p. 134–148). At the same time, the understanding that media is powerful appears to have become somewhat diffuse and widespread. In the context of social movements, researchers discerned that activists have also become "media savvy" (McCurdy, 2012, p. 249), developing "media strategies" (Rucht, 2004) and "lay theories of media" (McCurdy, 2011) that include knowledge about media's power, media's problems, how media works and so forth in order to take advantage of, negotiate or counter media power.

These studies either relate "media power" to "objective effects" or understand it as something mainly cognitive, as perception or knowledge. In this section, I would like to study media power in interaction. My argument is that media has power when people assume it has and act upon such assumptions during interactions. At the same time, interactions produce a situational frame, which includes definitions of the relationships, identities and speech norms at the scenes and which enables, constrains, modulates or reinforces such enactment.

"Media Power in Interaction" as a Case of "Culture in Interaction"

Trying to bridge the studies about "collective representations" and "cultural interactionism," Eliasoph and Lichterman (2003) developed an approach to study "culture in interaction." They start with an important insight from Goffman: when people come together, the first thing they ask implicitly is "what is going on here?" Eliasoph and Lichterman understand that people develop implicit understanding of situations through interactions (Goffman called them scene, frame or footing); these understandings relate to our collective representations, are of a limited number and inform and coordinate people's actions. Instead of studying multiple one-time encounters, Eliasoph and Lichterman study repeated interactions in autonomous, civic organizations that consist of similar composition of people for similar goals. They find that repeated interactions over time generate stable patterns, and these patterns constitute local cultures that interact with and filter the assumptions, language and symbols that individual participants bring to the gathering.

In their studies, Eliasoph and Lichterman (2003) and Lichterman and Eliasoph (2014) develop the concepts of "group style" or "scene styles" as heuristics to describe the local cultures. Group style or scene styles are concerned with multiple aspects of the shared understanding of "what is going on here," but three dimensions appear essential: One is a collectivity's implicitly shared "map" of reference points in the wider world—other groups, individuals, social categories—in relation to which participants draw their group's boundaries in the setting. Another is its group "bonds," or shared assumptions about obligations between members in the setting. The third is the "speech norms," or shared assumptions about the appropriate speech genres for a setting and the appropriate emotional tones to display there (Eliasoph & Lichterman, 2003, p. 739). To put it differently, group style or scene styles are concerned with identities (who are us and who are them), relationships (how do we relate to us and them) and appropriate ways of speaking and acting in interactions.

Following this line of thinking, I argue that studying "media-power-in-interaction" entails a three-step inquiry. We ask, first, what assumptions about media do people bring into their encounters? Second, how do people act upon these assumptions? Third, how do frames and scenes in local interactions influence people's media-oriented practices? Here, media is defined broadly, including the material devices such as camera, the acts of media use such as filming, and people who use the media devices, such as the press.

As Eliasoph and Lichterman (2003; Lichterman & Eliasoph, 2014) show, the "filtering" effects of local culture are particularly clear when repeated interactions have generated stable patterns overtime. In the current study, it is difficult, if not impossible, to find local interactional patterns that have stabilized. Nonetheless, by comparing multiple interactions, we could better understand how frame and scenes might influence the ways in which media assumptions are acted upon. Therefore, instead of focusing on one episode of interaction, I expand the dataset to include all three encounters between the applicants and Kim Davis in the Rowan County office recorded by someone friendly with the applicants and made available by David Moore on his YouTube channel (davidmoore 1976). In particular, for the third encounter, I mainly rely upon the second video provided by the preconference in 2016, as its documentation is longer and more comprehensive documentation.

Description and Analyses of Three Encounters

The First Encounter (July 7, 2015)

The encounter between the applicants and Kim Davis occurs towards the end of the first video (11:10). Almost instantly after they meet, Davis looks at the cameraperson, holds her palm up to indicate "stop" and says, "Well, I'd like you to put your phone away." The cameraperson responds, "It is his (David Moore's) rights to have it (the encounter) filmed as well." An unidentified male voice interjects, "It's also common courtesy not to shove it (the camera) in people's faces (11:21)." Another unidentified female voice adds, "It (not filming) is also for her (Kim Davis's) protection." The camera person states again, "It is also for his rights."

Kim Davis stares at the camera person and says, "We'll talk right here and you can, you can put that away. Okay?" She moves her palm up and down, indicating turning off of the phone. The cameraperson gives David Moore the phone: "David, here. Hold it yourself." David Moore takes over the phone and turns it down. The last sentence recorded in this video is Kim Davis saying, "You would . . . turn your recorder off."

Quickly after people come to meet face to face, different agents display divergent orientations to the use of media: the applicants adopt it, while Kim Davis and other people around her oppose it. Filming relates differently to people's map (how they relate to the outside world), bond (what are the obligations people have for ingroup members) and speech norms (what is the appropriate way of communicating in the setting). Underlying these disagreements and argumentations, however, is some shared, implicit assumption that media can be mobilized to do something or make a difference, otherwise Davis would not be adamant about turning it off, and Moore about recording. The divergence in media orientation and use, however, is quickly resolved, as Moore concedes and turns off the recording devices. By complying with the requests of respecting common courtesy and protecting Kim Davis, Moore participates in building and maintaining the suggested non-oppositional, "common courtesy" relationship in the interaction, even if such compliance also means compromising the applicants' pursuit of rights.

The Second Encounter (August 13, 2015)

The second video starts with the applicants talking to two deputy clerks outside of the office in the early morning. Moore and Ermold request that the deputy clerks issue marriage licenses, and the latter refuse. The applicants then accuse both the clerks of defying court injunctions. As the accusations pause, one deputy clerk smiles and says in an ironic way, "Good morning. We are not issuing marriage license today." The applicants respond with chortles, seemingly with ridicule and defiance. After a few less audible exchanges, David Moore asks, "We are not allowed to come in and film, because of why?" The deputy clerk hesitates shortly and answers, "Because our deputy clerks have requested not to be filmed this morning." The applicants then respond, "This is a public space." Later the applicants enter the office with their camera regardless, and the deputy clerks do not contest the act of filming any further.

In this encounter, the applicants and the clerks again have different media-oriented practices. While the applicants cite that "it is a public place" to legitimate filming, the deputy clerks cite their fellow deputies' request to disallow it. When the clerk responds to accusations with

"Good morning," it seems he tries to remind the applicants of common courtesy and maintain some interpersonal harmony in the setting. Nonetheless, the applicants are more interested in making their interactions confrontational, and they do so, among others, by continuing to videotape, even against the clerks' request, which reinforces the interactions' confrontational and antagonistic nature.

The Third Encounter (September 1, 2015)

In the third encounter, following the events that are part of the transcript used in this book's contributions, Kim Davis retreats to her office and closes the door, thus putting an end to her conversation with the applicants. Grudgingly, Moore goes to talk to two police officers, to no avail, and eventually turns around to the rallies, expressing obvious frustrations on his face and through words. A woman in a green shirt hugs Moore and comforts him (17:15), and more people follow suit. Moore opens up his hands and says, ironically, "There is no point for an injunction, because no one is gonna uphold it. What is the point of it? What is the point of any of it?" To this, a woman standing close to the wall responds with empowering messages that she has contacted ACLU and that they would file a motion of contempt against Davis. She says, "We have it all on video. She needs to go." People around her start cheering and clapping while David Moore responds with verbal and non-verbal expressions of acknowledgement and gratitude such as putting his hand on his chest, moving his lips as if he were saying "thank you," nodding and so forth.

In this setting, the bond of the situation prompts the applicants' supporters to offer comfort, encouragement and empowerment in the face of Moore's frustration. Hence the woman's explanation of a media strategy. This explanation reveals the assumption about media's power that the media recording will work together with the mobilization of civic organizations and legal procedures to challenge Davis's bureaucratic authority and decisions in a non-local context. While this assumption may have informed the woman's media practices, it is the scene, frame or relational dynamics from the interactions that have encouraged her to spell them out, thus reinforcing her positive orientation to media and even constituting another layer of media practice via performing the power of media. Just as Reed (2013) discerns, power could be performative when "its carrying through in social actions is like a speech act that threatens, pronounces, or promises," when "situated actions and interaction exerts control over actors and their future actions" (p. 203). While there is no guarantee in the setting that the assumed media power will realize, articulating the assumption and its according media strategy seem sufficient to comfort, cheer up and empower the applicants and supporters.

In all these interactions, the participants seemingly share some general assumptions that media has power, though they relate to the assumed media power in different ways. While some media orientations appear pre-formulated before people come to meet face to face, as interactions develop, considerations about relationships (map), identities (bond) and speech norms emerge and are negotiated in scenes, exerting influence on how people act upon their assumptions of media power. In conclusion, while media scholars might understand media power as objective effect or widely shared assumptions in contemporary society, in interaction, media's power depends on people's acting out of such assumption, and such enactments are influenced by dynamics of local interactions (frames or scenes).

Conversation Analysis (CA) and the Interactional Process of Constructing Authority

Nan Wang

Continuing our discussion of the accomplishment of authority among non-focal agents in the interaction, in this section, we want to bring our focus to the dyadic interaction between David Moore and the journalists and particularly to how the journalists, as a representative of the press, are being understood and oriented to by David Moore as having a certain amount of right and power in reaching a decision over issuing the marriage license to the Moore-Ermold couple. As shown in the video clip, during Moore and Davis's dispute, Moore is interrupted by several others whom he mistakes to be journalists. Despite this being a brief exchange, the interactional process, and in particular how the rights of taking turns to talk are distributed and negotiated between the relevant social actors, provides a prime analytical location to discuss the media's power and authority over the issue of marriage license issuance in this particular social encounter.

The analysis presented here is situated under the general debate of media power in society. On the one hand, media's representational power is considered one of society's main forces in its own right and an increasingly central dimension of power in contemporary societies (Melucci, 1996; Curran, 2002; Couldry & Curran 2003); on the other hand, many point out that media only "mediate" what goes on in society, that media power is only a term that people use to point to how other powerful forces use the intermediate mechanism of media (press reports, television coverage, websites, etc.) to wage their battles (Castells, 1997). Given that journalists constitute the largest number of participants present in this episode, it is natural to ask: what is the role of the press, and, specifically, how much power and authority does it have over the decision of the marriage license issuance? To answer this question, I analyze the interaction between David Moore and the journalists (lines 163–173 in the transcript) using a conversation analytic (CA) approach.

CA focuses on the systematic organization of social interaction through which participants' goals are accomplished and their relationships are constructed on a turn-by-turn and moment-by-moment basis (Heritage, 1984; Drew & Heritage, 1992). To CA analysts, an emphasis is not placed on how participants should act in interactions—what they say and how they say it based on their social roles or identities (i.e., gender, class, etc.)—but on how participants actually act—how they conform to or deviate from the normative expectations of their conducts (Pomerantz & Mandelbaum, 2004). Through examining the recurrent patterns of inter-actants' language practice, analysts form an empirical basis for their con-clusions of the type of social relations, hence the distribution of power and authority among the interactants. The analysis can be operated at several different levels, including turn-taking and turn allocation (Sacks, Schegloff, & Jefferson, 1974; Hayashi, 2012); organization of a sequence of turns (Schegloff, 2007; Stivers, 2012); and turn-design features (e.g., lexical choices, intonations, grammatical constructions of a turn) (Drew, 2012); as well as overall organization of some particular projected social activity (Robinson, 2012). Utilizing this analytic approach, I examine the role of the press, specifically its power and authority over the issuance of the Moore couple's marriage license.

Before starting, several contextual facts regarding this particular social encounter should be noted—its participants, their primary activity goal and their major challenge. The primary goal of the interaction is for Moore to obtain a marriage license from Davis, the county clerk, in order to marry his same-sex partner. The participants involve the couple, the county clerks, spectators and the press. Although the press forms the largest group of participants in this encounter, the interaction happens primarily between Davis and Moore. The primary challenge that the par-ticipants face is that Davis refuses to issue the license to the gay couple, although the Supreme Court has legalized same-sex marriage. The inter-action, thus, revolves around a negotiation of relative power between Davis and Moore, who put forward the authority of God as a religious institution and the authority of the Supreme Court as a government insti-tution, respectively, as mentioned in the earlier sections.

Through analyzing the interactional process between the press and the gay couple, and particularly by focusing on the turn-taking features of their interaction, it is argued that the press plays a marginal role in the decision-making of the issuance of the couple's marriage license. Three types of evidence are detailed below:

Evidence 1: Journalists Abandoning the Right to Talk

Although they are constantly present at the scene, journalists do not take turns to talk at all throughout the interactional activity. They limit their role to taking photos and video-recording the interaction between Kim Davis and the gay couple. The mere fact of the journalists' silent pres-ence displays their orientation to their own identity as an independent observer who has no control over the matter under discussion. In this sense, the journalists claim little right and power in participating in the decision regarding the marriage license.

Evidence 2: Journalists' Being Denied the Right to Talk

The journalists' participation is treated by David Moore, one of the primary participants to the interaction, as unwarranted and thus denied (as shown in the excerpt; see lines 163, 165, 168) in the decision-making process over the marriage license. In line 163, David Moore has mistaken the participating crowd to be part of the journalists and thereby asks them to "shut up"; this action of denying the other party's right to talk is then accounted for by David Moore by providing a rational ground in line 165, reasoning that he denies the crowd's right to talk on the basis that he believes the participating individuals are from the press (line 168). Therefore, the de-selection of the journalists' turn-taking rights clearly displays David Moore's orientation that the press has no right to participate in the decision of the matter. This provides further evidence that the press is oriented by the primary participants of the interaction as having a marginal role in decision-making over the marriage license.

Evidence 3: David Moore Granting Other Couples' Rights to Talk

At lines 171 and 173, once it is clarified that the other same-sex couple is not the press, David Moore immediately invites them to the front to make their statements and contribute their opinions regarding the marriage license issue (line 171, 173). Subsequently, these two crowd members are selected and granted the turn to talk and thus join the Moore couple as primary participants to the interaction. Thus, Moore's selection of the non-press individuals to talk demonstrate that other gay couples, rather than the journalists, are treated as having a similar amount of rights to talk and thus the ability and resources to influence the interactional outcome. This is in directly contrast with the press members, who are also part of the crowd.

In conclusion, through examining one aspect of the interactional process, that is, the turn-taking practices of the interactants, it is found that 1) the journalists do not actively take turns to talk and thus contribute minimally to the interaction, thus orienting to themselves as marginal in the decision-making process; 2) David Moore, the primary participant of the interaction, denies the journalists' right to take turns to talk, thus displaying his orientation to the press's marginal role in the decision-making process; and 3) in contrast, by granting another same-sex couple from the crowd the rights to talk, David Moore displays his orientation that other present members of the interaction (e.g., the other gay couple), rather than the press, have a more central role in this social encounter of requesting the issuance of a marriage license.

It should be noted that the findings of the analysis presented above do not mean that the press does not have any power or authority over the entire event of issuing the marriage license. What it does demonstrate is that the power and authority of media are not implemented through the local management of the interaction process; rather, their power and authority come from channels and mechanisms that go beyond the local interaction process of decision-making—such as social media campaigns and narrative production, which Yue Yang and Sky Marsen address.

Conclusion

In this chapter, we explored the concepts of authority and power as they relate to participants "on the sides," or the margin of the interaction between Davis and Moore. By doing so, we questioned the conventional framing of authority that draws attention to the exchange between two parties and, instead, proposed an approach for which authority is dynamic and fluid, constructed and negotiated in the interactions of different individuals and institutions, including those on whom attention is not immediately drawn. This is a view of authority as one that is fundamentally shared among actors, calling into question the idea that it can flow almost exclusively downward along the institutional hierarchy.

Authority has often been intimately linked to decision-making, and it appears as the legitimate power to decide (for a discussion of this trend see Benoit-Barné & Fox, 2017). For the approaches presented here, authority is more inclusive and diffuse. It entails the ability to create and challenge, through communication processes of various kinds, the very meaning attributed to the world. As such, exercising authority can be linked to decision-making, but it also implies being able to question, negotiate and co-create the meanings that constitute one's world (one's identities, roles, relationships, etc.). This consideration is important if we want to better understand and explain the local accomplishment as well as the social ramifications of social controversies such as the one under study.

In this regard, our analyses addressed key decisions that are at the heart of the Kim Davis controversy (in particular, Davis's decision to defy a court order and not issue marriage license to same-sex couples and Moore and Ermold's decision to release a video of Davis refusing to issue their marriage license). They also accounted for the participants' capacity to influence the meaning-making processes at stake both locally and with regard to the larger social significance of the interaction. As a result, we believe that decentering the analysis to account for a broader range of people and objects has allowed us to make explicit some of the ways in which decision-making and meaning-making are in fact intermingled

Table 6.1 Summary of Analytical Approaches to the authority of spectators, journalists, and others

Perspective	Authority as a relational effect of presence Chantal Benoit-Barné	Narrator's role in performing authority Sky Marsen	Media power in interaction Yue Yang	Conversation analysis Nan Wang
Analytical focus	We pay attention to the relations that are created and sustained as actors interact with each other.	We approach the text as a story with agents, their relationships and the events in which they interact.	I ask what people assume about media power, how these assumptions inform people's media-related practices and how these practices are enabled or constrained by local frames emergent from interactions.	CA focuses on the systematic organization of social interaction, through which participants' goals are accomplished and their relationships are constructed on a turn-by-turn and moment-by-moment basis.
How authority is constituted in interaction	Its local emergence and negotiation involve a process of presentification whereby established and recognizable entities are brought to bear on the interaction. It also entails a process of association and dissociation whereby actors create or negate relations.	The presenter of information, or narrator, orchestrates the actions by discursively positioning the different elements in ways that reflect the relations of authority among the characters in the story.	Media power is performed when people act with anticipation and assumptions about it. People enact power through language and practices, but situational frames emerging from and negotiated through interactions also enable, constrain or reinforce such enactment.	Authority is constructed and embodied in participants' design and use of social actions in interaction. Through analyzing recurrent patterns of language practice (such as turn design or sequential organization features), it reveals interactants' orientation to social norms and their understanding of their social relationship.
How it shifts understanding of authority	Authority is relational: it is a propriety of relationship (not of individuals or structures).	Authority is constructed in discourse and manifests in narrative structure.	Media has power when people assume it has and acts accordingly; at the same time, enactment of media power interacts with situational order.	Authority is constructed through an intersubjectivity process rather than a static property.

(Continued)

Table 6.1 (Continued)

Perspective	Authority as a relational effect of presence Chantal Benoit-Barné	Narrator's role in performing authority Sky Marsen	Media power in interaction Yue Yang	Conversation analysis Nan Wang
Key concepts	Author and authoring, presentification and effects of presence	Narrative and narrator, agents or characters	Media power, lay theory, enactment, culture in interaction, scene/frame, situation	Intersubjectivity, action formation
Suggested readings	Benoit-Barné and Cooren (2009), Taylor and Van Every (2014), and Benoit-Barné and Fox (2017)	Greimas (1987), Marsen (2006), Taylor, and Van Every (2015)	Eliasoph and Lichterman (2003), McCurdy (2011), and Reed (2017).	Sacks et al. (1974), Pomerantz and Mandelbaum (2004), and Heritage (1984)

in the establishment of authority, thus contributing to a more thorough understanding of the phenomenon.

All the approaches in this chapter agree that authority is a dynamic and fluid phenomenon that is constructed and negotiated in social interactions, even by agents that remain invisible, marginal or unspecified. Each perspective, however, differs in focus and emphasis. According to Benoit-Barné, authority is relational, emerging in social interaction through presentification, a communicative process by which agents co-create and negotiate the emergence of authority. For Marsen, authority is discursive, manifesting in the positioning of agents and the description of their actions and words by an orchestrating presenter, or narrator. In Yang's analysis, power and authority relates to widely shared assumptions (for instance, the idea of "media power"), but their enactment largely depends on situational construction of relationships and identities. Finally, Wang follows a conversation analytic approach that explicates how authority is socially constructed through interactants' exchange of social actions and their orientations toward the social relations embodied in their actions. Table 6.1 provides an overview of what characterizes the four approaches.

References

Bal, M. (1993). First person, second person, same person: Narrative as epistemology. *New Literary History*, 24, 293–320.

Barthes, R. (1977). *The death of the author*. Image/Music/Text (S. Heath, Trans., pp. 142–147). New York: Hill and Wang. (Original work published 1967).

Benoit-Barné, C., & Cooren, F. (2009). The accomplishment of authority through presentification: How authority is distributed among and negotiated by organizational members. *Management Communication Quarterly*, 23(1), 5–31.

Benoit-Barné, C., & Fox, S. (2017). Authority. In C. Scott & L. Lewis (Eds.), *The international encyclopedia of organizational communication*. New York: Wiley-Blackwell.

Bourdieu, P. (1991). *Language and symbolic power*. Cambridge, MA: Harvard University Press.

Breiger, R. L. (2000). A tool kit for practice theory. *Poetics*, 27(2–3), 91–115.

Cammaerts, B., Mattoni, A., & McCurdy, P. (Eds.). (2013). *Mediation and protest movements*. New York: Intellect Books.

Castells, M. (1997). *The power of identity*. Oxford, England: Blackwell.

Chatman, S. (1978). *Story and discourse: Narrative structure in fiction and film*. Ithaca, NY: Cornell University Press.

Cooren, F. (2006). The organizational world as a plenum of agencies. In F. Cooren, J. R. Taylor, & E. J. Van Every (Eds.), *Communication as organizing: Empirical and theoretical explorations in the dynamic of text and conversation* (pp. 81–100). Mahwah, NJ: Lawrence Erlbaum.

Cooren, F., Brummans, H. J. M., & Charrieras, D. (2008). The coproduction of organizational presence: A study of Médecins Sans Frontières in action. *Human Relations*, 61(10), 1339–1370.

Couldry, N. (2001). The hidden injuries of media power. *Journal of Consumer Culture, 1*(2), 155–177.

Couldry, N. (2002). *The place of media power: Pilgrims and witnesses of the media age.* London: Routledge.

Couldry, N., & Curran, J. (Eds.). (2003). *Contesting media power: Alternative media in a networked world.* Boulder, CO: Rowman & Littlefield.

Couldry, N., & Hepp, A. (2013). Conceptualizing mediatization: Contexts, traditions, arguments. *Communication Theory, 23*(3), 191–202.

Curran, J. (2002). *Media and power.* London: Routledge.

Drew, P. (2012). Turn design. In *The handbook of conversation analysis* (pp. 131–149). Oxford, UK: Wiley-Blackwell. https://doi.org/10.1002/9781118325001.ch7

Drew, P., & Heritage, J. (1992). *Talk at work: Interaction in institutional settings.* Cambridge, UK: Cambridge University Press.

Eliasoph, N., & Lichterman, P. (2003). Culture in interaction. *American Journal of Sociology, 108*(4), 735–794.

Genette, G. (1983). *Narrative discourse: An essay in method.* (J. E. Lewin, Trans.). New York: Cornell University Press. (Original work published 1978).

Greimas, A. J. (1987). *On meaning: Selected writings in semiotic theory.* (P. J. Perron & F. H. Collins, Trans.). Minneapolis, MN: University of Minnesota Press. (Original work published 1983).

Gumbrecht, H. U. (2004). *Production of presence: What meaning cannot convey.* Stanford, CA: Stanford University Press.

Hayashi, M. (2012). Turn allocation and turn sharing. In J. Sidnell & T. Stivers (Eds.), *The handbook of conversation analysis* (pp. 167–190). Oxford, UK: Wiley-Blackwell. https://doi.org/10.1002/9781118325001.ch9

Heritage, J. (1984). *Garfinkel and ethnomethodology.* Cambridge, UK: Polity Press.

Herman, D. (2009). *Basic elements of narrative.* Oxford, UK: Wiley Blackwell.

Jahn, M. (2001). Narrative voice and agency in drama: Aspects of a narratology of drama. *New Literary History, 32*, 659–679.

Lichterman, P., & Eliasoph, N. (2014). Civic action. *American Journal of Sociology, 120*(3), 798–863.

Livingstone, S. (2009). On the mediation of everything: ICA presidential address 2008. *Journal of communication, 59*(1), 1–18.

Marsen, S. (2006). *Narrative dimensions of philosophy.* London: Palgrave.

McCurdy, P. (2011). Theorizing lay theories of media: A case study of the dissent! Network at the 2005 Gleneagles G8 Summit. *International Journal of Communication, 5*, 619–638.

McCurdy, P. (2012). Social movements, protest and mainstream media. *Sociology Compass, 6*(3), 244–255.

Melucci, A. (1996). *Challenging codes: Collective action in the information age.* Cambridge, UK: Cambridge University Press.

Pomerantz, A., & Mandelbaum, J. (2004). Conversation analytic approaches to the relevance and uses of relationship categories in interaction. In K. L. Fitch & R. E. Sanders (Eds.), *Handbook of language and social interaction.* New York, NY: Routledge Handbooks Online. https://doi.org/10.4324/9781410611574.ch6

Prince, G. (2003). Surveying narratology. In T. Kindt & H.-H. Muller (Eds.), *What is narratology? Questions and answers regarding the status of a theory* (pp. 1–16). Berlin and New York: Walter de Gruyter.

Reed, I. A. (2013). Power: Relational, discursive, and performative dimensions. *Sociological Theory*, *31*(3), 193–218.

Reed, I. A. (2017). Chains of power and their representation. *Sociological Theory*, *35*(2), 87–117.

Robinson, J. D. (2012). Overall structural organization. In *The handbook of conversation analysis* (pp. 257–280). New York: Wiley-Blackwell. https://doi.org/10.1002/9781118325001.ch13

Rucht, D. (2004). The quadruple "A": Media strategies of protest movements since the 1960s. In W. van De Donk, B. Loader, P. Nixon, & D. Rucht (Eds.), *Cyberprotest: New media, citizens and social movements* (pp. 29–56). London: Routledge.

Sacks, H., Schegloff, E., & Jefferson, G. (1974). A simplest systematics for the organization of turn-taking for conversation. *Language*, *50*, 696–735.

Schegloff, E. (2007). *Sequence organization in interaction: A primer in conversation analysis*. Cambridge: Cambridge University Press.

Stivers, T. (2012). Sequence organization. In *The handbook of conversation analysis* (pp. 191–209). New York: Wiley-Blackwell. https://doi.org/10.1002/9781118325001.ch10

Taylor, J., & Van Every, E. J. (2014). *When organization fails: Why authority matters*. New York: Routledge.

Thompson, J. B. (1995). *The media and modernity: A social theory of the media*. Palo Alto, CA: Stanford University Press.

Appendix
Transcript of County Clerk Defying Supreme Court on Gay Marriage

Video available at www.youtube.com/watch?v=ComaDQijgxA
An alternate version is available at https://youtu.be/T7HNVEQ4OmU?t=376
This transcription is inspired by the method suggested by Gail Jefferson (2004) and which has come to be known as the Jeffersonian transcription convention. It allows to capture not only *what* is being said but also *how*.

For the purpose of this transcript, we use the following special symbols:

- ((double parentheses)) are used to describe non-verbal aspects of what goes on;
- (.) (0.5) single parentheses with a dot or with a number in them indicate a brief pause of either a tenth of a second or the duration the numbers designate in seconds;
- = equal signs at the end of a turn of talk and at the beginning of the next indicate that there was no break or gap between them;
- A dash- following a word signals a cut-off or an unfinished word;
- [opening square brackets indicate where an overlap begins, with the aligned square brackets in the next line;
- ↑ an upward arrow corresponds to a higher pitch, as is the case when ending a question, for instance;
- > right and left carats < bracket a portion of the talk that is speeded up;
- Colu:::ms indicate the preceding sound is prolongated;
- Underlined words are stressed;
- UPPERCASE words are told louder than normal, as when shouting;
- (xxx), (inaudible) or (word) indicate that the transcriber could not understand what was said or that there is uncertainty about that was actually said.

Reference

Jefferson, G. (2004). Glossary of transcript symbols with an introduction. In G. H. Lerner (Ed.), *Conversation analysis: Studies from the first generation* (pp. 13–31). Amsterdam and Philadelphia: John Benjamins Publishing Company.

1	ERMOLD	absolu↑tely ludicrous ((Kim Davis arrives from her office. She is smiling))
2		(1.0)
3	ERMOLD	Don't smile at [me
4	MOORE	[Here she is
5		(0.5)
6	DAVIS	I did not smile
7		(2.0)
8	DAVIS	I'm not being disrespectful to you ((shaking her head))
9	ERMOLD	You absolu[tely have disrespected us
10	MOORE	[You absolutely are, treating us as second-class citizens=
11	DAVIS	=[No I don't ((shaking her head))
12	MOORE	=[is what you are doing, telling us that we don't deserve the same right rights
13		that you do think that you have
14	DAVIS	I'm saying that [you do-
15	MOORE	[and even though in your entire life-
16		(0.5)
17	MOORE	Would you do this to an interracial couple?
18		(2.0)
19	DAVIS	A man and a woman, no↑ ((smiling))
20		(2.0) ((Moore nods his head))
21	MOORE	How many times have you been married, Kim?
22		(0.5)
23	DAVIS	I just want you all to know that we are not issuing marriage licenses to[day=
24	OTHER	[Why
25	DAVIS	=pending
26		(0.5)
27	DAVIS	[Hum
28	WOMAN	[(((yelling)) contempt to court
29	MOORE	What appeal is left?=
30	DAVIS	=Pending the appeal of [the Sixth Circuit↑
31	ERMOLD	[It's been denied
32		(0.3)
33	ERMOLD	[What's the appeal on the Sixth Circuit?
34	DAVIS	[The appeal <u>stay</u> has been denied ((nodding))
35	MOORE	Right=
36	DAVIS	=[So
37	MOORE	[The induction is the order is that you are supposed to issue marriage li[censes
38	DAVIS	[And
39		we are not issuing marriage [licenses today.
40	MOORE	[The Supreme Court denied your stay
41	DAVIS	We are not issuing marriage licenses today [sir
42	MOORE	[Based on what?
43	DAVIS	I would ask you all [to- [go ahead and-
44	MOORE	[Why are you [not issuing marriage licenses today?
45		(0.5)
46	DAVIS	Because (.) I'm not
47	ERMOLD	Under [whose authority? (0.5) are you not issuing [licenses?
48	MOORE	[Why
49	DAVIS	[Under God's authority
50		((looking defiantly at David Ermold))

51   OTHER   Did the lawyers tell you-
52   MOORE   [Did God tell you to do this? Did God tell you how to treat us (.) like this?
53   ERMOLD   [I don't believe in your god. I don't believe in your god. I don't believe in
54   your [god
55   DAVIS   [((looking at Moore)) I've asked you all to leave, you are interrupting
56   [my business ((opening her arms))
57   MOORE   [You can call the police if you want us to leave
58   OTHER   It's not your business
59   MOORE   You can call the police.
60   OTHER   It's the Rowan County
61   DAVIS   [That's exactly right people can't get in here ((speaking to this person on her
62   left))
63   MOORE   [I'm paying you your salary ((repeatedly pointing his index at her))
64   (0.5)
65   MOORE   I PAY YOUR SALARY ((repeatedly pointing his index at her and raising his
66   voice))
67   ((Kim Davis makes a look expressing a form of surprise))
68   OTHER   We pay your salary
69   MOORE   I pay you to discriminate against me right now ((Banging hand against the
70   counter)) that's what I'm paying for
71   ((Kim Davis reacts with a look implying "too bad for you"))
72   MOORE   ((looking at his partner)) that's what I'm paying for. I'm paying↑ (.) for this
73   memory (.) with my partner that >I love, that I have been with for seventeen
74   years<. ((flapping on the counter this his right hand)) What's the longest you've
75   been with someone, that you've been married to someone?
76   ERMOLD   [((laughs))
77   DAVIS   [I'm asking you to lea:::ve.
78   MOORE   I'm not leaving
79   (.)
80   DAVIS   Okay, you all [so you could just push back away ((making a gesture with both
81   hands, imitating the action of pushing))
82   ERMOLD   [I'm asking you to do your job
83   DAVIS   [You are all welcome to stay
84   MOORE   [I'm not leaving
85   MOORE   I'm not leaving
86   DAVIS   [Just push back away from the counter
87   MOORE   [can't help with the pressure, here (.) no
88   ERMOLD   No, no
89   DAVIS   Just push back [away from the counter
90   ERMOLD   [We're not leaving until we have a license. (.) We're not
91   leav[ing until we have a license
92   DAVIS   [Then you're gonna have a long day.
93   OTHER   Do your job!
94   DAVIS   Good day ((leaves while waving the crowd with her left hand))
95   MOORE   We will call the police. I will ask them to arrest you
96   OTHER   Do your job! Do your job! Do your job
97   MOORE   CALL THE POLICE
98   (0.3) ((Kim waves the crowd with her right hand while getting in her office)
99   MOORE   CALL THE POLICE ((pointing his finger at her while she is leaving)), GO

100		AHEAD [I will ask them to arrest you
101		[(*applause)*
102	OTHER	Do your job!
103	OTHER	Coward
104	MOORE	YOU SHOULD BE ASHAMED OF YOURSELF↑ ((pointing his finger in her
105		direction while she is closing her door)),
106		(0.5)
107	MOORE	EVERYONE IN THIS OFFICE SHOULD BE ASHAMED OF
108		THEMSELVES ((pointing at all the employees and banging on the counter
109		with his right hand when saying "ashamed"))
110		(0.5) ((Ermold puts his right hand on Moore's left shoulder))
111	MOORE	IS THIS WHAT YOU WANT TO REMEMBER? ((pointing to one of the
112		employees and then knocking his fist on the counter))
113		(0.5)
114	MOORE	IS THIS WHAT YOU WANT TO REMEMBER ((pointing to one of the
115		employees and then knocking his fist on the counter. Ermold removes his hand
116		from Moore's left shoulder)) THAT YOU STOOD UP FOR THIS? ((knocking
117		again his fist on the counter))
118		(1.0)
119	OLD CLERK	Amen, yes sir ((pointing his right index to the ceiling))
120	MOORE	THAT YOUR CHILDREN WILL HAVE TO LOOK AT YOU ((knocking his
121		fist on the counter when saying "children")) AND REALIZE THAT YOU
122		ARE BIGOTS ((knocking his fist on the counter when saying "bigots"))
123		((Kim David gets out of her office and comes back to the counter))
124	MOORE	AND THAT YOU DISCRIMINATED AGAINST PEOPLE? ((knocking his
125		fist on the counter when saying "discriminated"))
126	OLD CLERK	No, no [discrimination
127	MOORE	[is that what you want of- [Is that what you want?
128	OLD CLERK	[We're praying for God and God's word and
129		find solace= ((raising his right hand toward the ceiling))
130	ERMOLD	=God (.) [does not belong in the county clerk's office ((bending toward Kim
131		Davis as she is getting back to them))
132	OTHER	[God doesn't run the government!
133	OTHER	God doesn't run the government!
134		((Kim Davis is back in front of Ermold and Moore))
135	OTHER	This is not a house of God!
136	MOORE	Call them, call the police (xxx). Call them now. ((Hits hand on the counter)).
137	DAVIS	[It's what you [are- David
138	MOORE	[SOMEBODY CALL THEM
139	ERMOLD	Call them
140	DAVIS	[David, listen to me
141	MOORE	[Call them call them I'm beyond listening to you ((with a tone of exasperation))
142		(0.3)
143	MOORE	This is [ridiculous
144	DAVIS	[David, please, [I'm asking you, please listen to me=
145	OTHER	[Do your job
146	MOORE	=I don't- I don't care how polite you are-
147	OTHER	We've heard [you
148	MOORE	[Or what you [feel::=

149	OTHER	[We've heard you
150	DAVIS	=I know you don't care
151		(0.5)
152	MOORE	You're [not- this is not [polite
153	DAVIS	[This is- [this is- [This is what I want to do
154	MOORE	[I would never do this to someone, what you
155		are doing to us, I would never (.) do to someone=
156	DAVIS	=You believe passionately in wh[at you are doing as I do ((making a circle
157		with her hands))
158	MOORE	[You do not understand what you are doing to
159		people
160	DAVIS	Okay?=
161	PARTNER 2	=But [you're forcing religion on other people
162	DAVIS	[As I do
163	MOORE	((Turning towards crowd)) Can you guys shut up?
164		(1.0)
165	MOORE	You're the press, so shut up.
166	PARTNER 1	No we're waiting for a [license too
167	PARTNER 2	[Yeah, we're waiting for a license
168	MOORE	((turning towards the two other partners)) I'm sorry ((flapping his two hands on
169		the counter)) I thought it was the press
170		((laughter))
171	MOORE	You guys come up here too!
172		(0.5)
173	MOORE	Come up here (.) tell them, (.) tell them, [tell them to their face.
174	DAVIS	[I'm alright
175	PARTNER 1	She's already denied it a couple times last, so.
176	PARTNER 2	This is your job mam, that's all we are asking. Do your job, but you have
177		another option, you can step down
178		(1.0)
179	PARTNER 2	If your beliefs mean that much to you, resign::: ↑
180		(1.0)
181	PARTNER 2	But does $80,000 [a year mean more to you than your beliefs.
182	MOORE	[((answering to his partner)): no, I am not going to calm
183		down and I'm not leaving
184	DAVIS	No my beliefs cannot be separated from me I [cannot take my hat off in my=
185	ERMOLD	[Then you should quit
186	DAVIS	=(xxxx[xxxxxxxxxxxxxxxxxxxxxxxxxxxxxxxxxxxxxx)
187	PARTNER 2	[Then you should quit! Then you should quit
188	DAVIS	((Turning towards Ermold and looking at him defiantly)) Why should I have to
189	PARTNER 1	You force your religion on us!
190	ERMOLD	Why? Are- are- are you saying [that our lives are worth your $80,000 a year
191	MOORE	[I would quit if I [was forced to do something
192		that I would not believe. I would quit my job
193	DAVIS	[I'm not saying your lives are
194		not worth- I hm- You are putting words in my mouth↓ and that will not do. I
195		simply told you all, I'm willing to face my consequences and you will all face
196		your consequences when it comes time for judgment=
197	MOORE	=We don't have conse[quences I don't believe in your judgment

198	DAVIS	[It's plain and simple
199	PARTNER 2	Not everyone believes [the way you believe
200	MOORE	[Not everyone believes what you believe=
201	DAVIS	=That's your choice, [that's your choice
202	MOORE	[you're creating a religion in this office-
203	DAVIS	No I'm [not ((shaking her head))
204	PARTNER 2	[Yes you are
205	MOORE	[xxx
206	PARTNER 2	You are making yourself a figurehead of this (.) new (.) church, here
207	MOORE	This is not the 1960s=
208	DAVIS	=It's-=
209	MOORE	=This is not-
210	DAVIS	[Jesus is the same today, yesterday, and forever ((bending toward David
211		Moore)
212	PARNER 2	[You're forcing your religion on your workers
213	OTHER	[(xxx) in the name of God.
214	MOORE	I don't (.) Do you even know our religious beliefs are? You know why? You
215		don't need to know, we don't need to know [yours↑
216	DAVIS	[Exactly that's ok, that's ok
217	MOORE	You can [have whatever beliefs you want
218	DAVIS	[That's ok [that's your choice
219	MOORE	[I believe you should have the right to have whatever
220		beliefs [you want. Absolutely
221	DAVIS	[That's- (.) Exactly, exac[tly= ((raising her finger in Moore's direction))
222	MOORE	[You have the right to your [beliefs ((banging
223		mildly his right first on the counter twice))
224	DAVIS	[Exactly, so if
225		what [you all are trying to accomplish=
226	MOORE	[You don't have the right to take our rights away based on your beliefs.
227	DAVIS	=is to get a mar[riage license you can go anywhere in the surrounding areas
228		((making a circle around herself with her two hands))
229	MOORE	[We are trying to get a marriage license and we are going to
230		stay until you give it to us
231	PARTNER 2	We do not have to go to another county=
232	DAVIS	=You don't live in Rowan County ((pointing toward Partner 2 with the palm of
233		her right hand))
234	PARTNER 2	We do- [we do (xxxx) here
235	MOORE	[It's legal in our county
236	DAVIS	That's ok, that's ok
237		((confusion from 4:31 to 4:35))
238	ERMOLD	Let me ask you one question
239	DAVIS	We're done here
240	ERMOLD	No please, let me ask you one question
241	DAVIS	We're done
242	ERMOLD	One question
243	DAVIS	If you want-
244	MOORE	It's gonna take five years to sue you, [that's all it's gonna take (.) out of my life
245	ERMOLD	[David, let me ask her a question
246	MOORE	I don't want that

247	ERMOLD	Let me ask her a question
248	DAVIS	I don't want you to be put out anymore that, I don't [want to be put out
249		any more than that
250	ERMOLD	[will you please let me ask
251		her a question
252	MOORE	Ask her a question
253		(0.5)
254	ERMOLD	Yo[u have one deputy clerk
255	DAVIS	[There is a remedy, there is a remedy to this
256	ERMOLD	I I would like to ask you a question
257	DAVIS	If the governor would do what he is supposed to do, he could settle all this

Index

Note: Page numbers in bold indicate tables on the corresponding pages.

Printed in the United States
by Baker & Taylor Publisher Services